ALBERT WILLIAM LEVI is David May Distinguished University Professor of the Humanities at Washington University and author of *Philosophy and the Modern World* (for which he received the first Ralph Waldo Emerson Award from Phi Beta Kappa), *Literature, Philosophy, and the Imagination,* and *Humanism and Politics.* He has received the Silver Medal Pro Meritus from the University of Graz, and is a member of the National Council of the Humanities.

THE HUMANITIES TODAY

The Humanities Today

ALBERT WILLIAM LEVI

❦ ❦ ❦

INDIANA UNIVERSITY PRESS

Bloomington & London

To

LAWRENCE WALTER
(June 28, 1968)
a very little book
for
a very little boy

CONTENTS

PREFACE

This little book owes its genesis to an invitation of Professor A. Robert Caponigri to deliver five short lectures to a workshop in the humanities at the University of Notre Dame on the topic "Contemporary Problems in the Humanities." The following are those lectures almost exactly as delivered in June 1968, without any attempt to disguise their informal and provisional character.

In the week prior to my own appearance, Professor Richard McKeon of the University of Chicago gave five lectures to the Notre Dame Workshop on the topic "The History of the Humanities As a Unified Field," and my lectures were meant to follow his historical account with a "problems" approach. Although I was not privileged to hear Professor McKeon's lectures, occasional reference to them in the following pages represents an attempt to maintain a certain continuity in our joint humanistic concern.

The participants in the workshop were all teachers of the humanities at Notre Dame, recruited from the languages and literatures, history, and philosophy; and under the able leadership of Professor Caponigri their questions and comments were in themselves eminently rewarding. I should like here to thank both them and Professor Caponigri for a week of delightful and illuminating humanistic discussion.

But I think that the questions herein raised are more far-reaching than those of any merely local institution, and it is for this reason that in an age so needy of the services which the humanities can render, I offer them for the consideration of a wider audience.

ALBERT WILLIAM LEVI

Vienna, May 2, 1969

THE HUMANITIES TODAY

INTRODUCTION

What are *the humanities,* and what is their future? The more intensively one is led to consider these questions, the more puzzled one becomes, for the matter of their definition and delimitation has been hopelessly confused by the accidents of their history, and the security of their future has in our time been vehemently challenged by the claims of newer and more clamorous disciplines—by the venturesome natural sciences and by the imperialistically inclined social arts.

Is it true that the humanities, once the province of the gentleman and the gentlemanly scholar, are irrelevant in the age of the technician and the professional? Or is it the case that as the custodian of values, and taking the realm of value experience as their rightful domain, they are the permanent prophets of the utopian future and the eternal agents of a recall to individual virtue and social order which no epoch dare conveniently ignore? Are the contemporary humanities living up to their claims that they "teach values," or have they become so corrupted by professionalism, so overimpressed by the newer scientific tools of cataloguing, storage, and retrieval—by statistical techniques, microfilms, and computers—that their chief preoccupations have made them monuments of linguistic and historical irrelevance, worthy in literal fact to be called today what the Middle Ages called them with local pride—the "trivial arts"?

Each practitioner of the humanities must answer these insistent questions for himself, and since for the past few years they have been of increasing theoretical and practical concern to me personally, I am grateful for the opportunity to set down a few of my ideas here. As one whose chief professional concern is the history and philosophy of culture and the history of ideas, I consider myself to be a philosopher of the humanities as others consider themselves philosophers of science or of the law. As one interested in logic and conceptual order, I have long been disturbed by the confusions in terminology and the setting of boundaries which afflict the field of the humanities. As a member of the rather recently constituted (1966) National Council of the Humanities, I have had to wrestle with practical policy issues in the humanities at the national level which cry out for clearer guidelines in theory than we have possessed. The lectures which follow reflect this triple concern. If I were to characterize their stance, their point of view, their philosophic base, I should say that they are an attempt to do justice to, and to reconcile, the competing claims of history, of logic, and of practice.

History as such was surely not my primary concern. But past and present form one seamless web, and present problems are often only the legacy of past history. Certainly this is true of the humanities. For anyone who attempts to define the humanities today finds to his confusion and dismay a sharp opposition between two distinct conceptions: one holding that they are skills or techniques, or "ways of doing" or *arts*; the other, that they are fields or areas of attention or "contents" or *subject matters*. The first is the enduring legacy of the Middle Ages; the second, that of the Renaissance.

From the first century before Christ (when Varro was writing his lost treatises on the liberal arts) to Martianus Capella in the fourth century A.D. the tradition of "the seven liberal arts" was being slowly established, finally to be given definitive status by Cassiodorus and Isidore of Seville in the two centuries following.[1] That the trivial arts of grammar, rhetoric, and dialectic were skills to be taught was self-evident, and even the quadrivium—arithmetic, geometry, astronomy, and music (the first three of which we should today term *sciences*)—were presented as practical arts. Arithmetic, usually discussed in connection with the abacus was "the art of calculating." Geometry, often indistinguishable from geography, was practically equated with surveying and remained close to its etymology as "earth-measurement." Even astronomy was intimately related to the practical problems of the fixing of the calendar and the computation of the date of Easter. These conceptions lasted well into the fourteenth century.

The radical revision of Renaissance education shifts the center of focus in such a way that arts are imperceptibly transformed into subject matters. Logic, not originally burdened with metaphysical problems, became so increasingly in the course of the late Middle Ages. The Renaissance and Enlightenment distinction between natural, metaphysical, and moral philosophy augmented subject-matter concern. The emergent nationalisms gave to history a new thematic importance, and the rise of the vernacular languages and their literary products turned the philological emphasis of grammar further in the direction of the investigation and study of literary content. Not the seven liberal arts, but the languages and literatures, history, and philosophy have become increasingly the claimants for humanistic attention.

It will be seen from my own attempts at definition in the first lecture that, although I take as my chief data the obvious subject-matter preference which marks contemporary education, I do not wish to abandon the tradition of the liberal arts. I have, therefore, identified the humanities with the liberal arts, but so redefined the latter (as the arts of communication, continuity, and criticism) as to make the humanities essentially coincide with the languages and literatures, history, and philosophy. This is a compromise, but one wholly in line with the demands of current practice.

I have thus been able to preserve the basic distinction between the sciences and the arts and to divide each of these areas respectively into the natural and the social sciences, the liberal and the fine arts. But a definition is only a conceptual tool. It is not an impassable frontier. Some of the most crucial questions in the contemporary philosophy of education hinge on the grounds of distinction between the sciences and the arts,[2] and some of the most perplexing dilemmas result from the partial overlap of the humanities and the social sciences and of the humanities and the fine arts.

To make distinctions and then to explore their inadequacy is the mark of a reasonable philosophic sophistication. Sometimes I have emphasized the distinctions; sometimes their inadequacies. When it is a matter of *method*, the boundary between the arts and the sciences becomes more relevant. When it is a question of *values*, all of the intellectual disciplines tend to unite in a vast continuum, and boundaries become vague and inconclusive. What we have here is the educational variant of the ancient Platonic problem of "the one and the many"—of sameness and difference. At one moment I stress the likeness between the intellectual disciplines; at another, their differences. This, I am afraid, gives to the following lectures an ineradicably dialectical character. But only the strictest of logicians will be dissatisfied with this procedure. It was Carnap, I think, who said of Nicolai Hartmann: "Every time Hartmann makes an elementary mistake in formal logic, he thinks he has discovered another antinomy." I understand his impatience. But if there are antinomies here, it is not simply because the proprieties of formal logic have not been observed. The humanities lend themselves to just such varieties of comparison.

Above all, it should not be thought that a clear demarcation of subject matter implies its total isolation in the educational process. This was the issue which distinguished the educational philosophies of President Robert M. Hutchins and Professor Alfred North Whitehead thirty years ago,[3] and much as I have admired President Hutchins's emphasis upon clarity and order, I have been no less an admirer of Professor Whitehead's insistence upon suggestiveness and the necessity for a mutual interpenetration of the different faculties within the modern university. In this very connection, there will probably be some who are surprised, if not shocked, to find that in my scheme the fine arts are not an intrinsic part of the humanities. This is because I see an important difference between "knowledge" and "creativity" which should have its expression in the distinction between the "fine" and the "liberal" arts. But to see how they differ is not to deny that they both belong within the structure of the university and that they should be taught side by side with a constant mutual reference.

But to define the humanities is only the first and most preliminary of my purposes. I have tried also to deal with that most eminent of clichés—that while the sciences teach facts and generalizations about facts, the humanities "teach values." The cliché is based on truth, but when one examines its grounds, it is by no means as obvious as it is sometimes thought to be, and when one compares (as I have found it only honest to do) the excessive claims made by the partisans of the humanities with the actualities of current humanities practice, the cliché becomes the basis of an invitation to present reform rather than a mere certification of past nobility. It would be less than candid to make no mention of the fact that the humanities, for all their vested rights and privileges in the structure of traditional education, are under heavy attack today.[4] Critics from C. P. Snow to William Arrowsmith have found them morally irresponsible and arrogant, when not actually trivial and irrelevant. But just as a pessimist is frequently a man who has to live with an optimist, so the cynics of the humanities are often those who have been romanticists in the humanities too young. Any gap between excessive claims and modest performance breeds bitter criticism, and no one who has intimate acquaintance with current performance in the humanities—whether at the level of teaching or research—can fail to see how far they have fallen short of, for example, the moral seriousness of an Erasmus or the political relevance of a Schiller. But this is precisely what must be first spoken of and acknowledged by all lovers of the humanities. Their very indispensibility points out the crying need for their inevitable reform.

In these lectures issues of values, of social context, of ultimate aims, loom large. But underlying them all, like "the ghost in the machine" is the basic intellectual problem of our age—the antagonism between the humanities and the sciences. To this problem, dramatized for our generation by C. P. Snow's concept of "the two cultures," I have devoted the third lecture, "Knowledge." Whatever of basic theory appears in these lectures (apart from the definitions of lecture one) is to be found here. For my distinction between the vocabulary of the humanities and the vocabulary of the sciences—what I have called "the scientific chain of meaning" in contradistinction to "the humanistic complex"—represents a long-standing conviction that the human imagination presents quite different tasks and creates quite different cultural products than the human understanding. This belief, which in the end constitutes a kind of philosophical rationale for the humanities, I have presented elsewhere in greater detail,[5] but its recurrence here probably saves these lectures from constituting simply *un livre de circonstance*. The specific topics which I treat are current, immediate, and pressing, but my treatment of them is grounded in a philosophical position to which I have long adhered.

1 ❖ Definition

FROM THE INTELLECTUAL HISTORY OF WESTERN EUROPE IT
IS POSSIBLE TO DERIVE AN UNBROKEN TRADITION IN THE HUMANITIES
with which her present practitioners can identify and which must
be to us a source of unending pride. The Platonic Academy with
its Pythagorean faith that mathematics is somehow the source of
principles of moral and aesthetic value; the Roman rhetorical impulse which allied persuasion to the pursuit of moral virtue and
the aims of the responsible commonwealth; the conservative labors
of early monasticism lovingly transcribing the great works of pagan
culture to outlast a time of troubles; the twelfth century cathedral
schools of Orleans and Chartres for whom grammatical analysis was
but a labor of love performed upon the enduring texts to aid in the
extraction of the beauty and wisdom which they contained; the
courts of Rimini and Urbino, mingling the ghost of Plato with the
essentials of decorous behavior and the development of character;
the flowering of Oxford and Cambridge from the days of Thomas
More to the time of John Locke, where the Greek and Roman
classics were used to humanize the law and to provide a kind of
magnanimous foundation for the national civil service; the renaissance of the study of ancient history at the University of Berlin in
the nineteenth century to provide the metaphors and the examples
for Prussian unification as the resurgence of philology at Vienna
during the same time serviced those linguistic talents necessary for
the administration of a polyglot Hapsburg empire—all reinforce our
faith in humanistic excellence and reassure us, living today in an era
of scientific dominance, that the humanities were not always considered trivial and irrelevant to issues of moral perplexity and political concern. We forge for ourselves, as I say, an unbroken tradition with which we may identify with pride.

And yet below the unitary surface of this tradition there may be other memories which make us faintly uneasy—memories of conflict, discord, and exploitation. Socrates waged an ironic war against the Sophists. Plato's transcendental axiology does not accord with Aristotle's pragmatic account of moral development. The early thirteenth century witnessed a "battle of the seven liberal arts" in which not religion but logic as represented by the University of Paris smothered the classical renaissance of the twelfth century, only itself to be vanquished almost three hundred years later by the rhetorical flourishes of Ramus and the new power of Cartesian science. In fact, it is not easy to forget that practically throughout their entire history there has been some kind of opposition between the arts and the sciences. This antagonism, which existed as early as the time of Boccaccio and Chrysoloras, between the protagonists of the newly acquired Arabic natural science on the one hand and the humanist sponsors of the classical revival on the other, gradually increased in virulence. For if the Middle Ages and the early Renaissance were the great ages of the humanities, the nineteenth century was the golden period of natural science, and if during this time Windelband and Rickert, Dilthey and Simmel, find it necessary to distinguish between the *Naturwissenschaften* and the *Geistewissenschaften*, this is essentially a defensive move of the philosophers of culture against the magnificent accomplishments of Faraday and Boltzmann, Clerk Maxwell and Virchow, Dalton and Johannes Mueller.

But my theme here is not the issue of the two cultures which C. P. Snow has so well dramatized for our consciousness. I will return to that in a subsequent lecture on the problem of humanistic knowledge. But now my concern is rather that of the definition of the humanities which has become increasingly difficult as we pass from ancient Greece and Rome to Renaissance Florence and London, and from Renaissance Florence and London to nineteenth century Berlin and Göttingen and present-day Chicago and Harvard. The chief characteristics which the humanities have had in the past, "their history as a unified field," as Professor McKeon calls it, despite its changing conditions and local variation, hinges upon a series of concepts which have an admirable simplicity. The "Greek and Roman classics," which worked toward the education of taste, the development of the moral person, even toward the production of that ineffable quality which we term *wisdom*, were once the entire curriculum of European education. The "seven liberal arts," comprising the sciences of harmony and measure as well as measurement and the "trivial" skills of textual interpretation, linguistic persuasiveness, and analytic judgment were pointed toward the disciplining of mind in all the possible modes of its occurrence so that the literary experience with its aesthetic appeal, its moral relevance, and its possible political applicability could rightfully be directed not toward a fragmented center but toward *a whole man.*

But the societal integration, or, as some sociologists have it, the relatively parochial outlook, which made the conception of this "wholeness" possible has disintegrated under the impact of the rise of the vernacular languages and literatures, the emergence of nationalism, the growth of industrial technology, and the loss of undisputed authoritativeness by a single intellectual elite possessing a monopoly of the instruments of philosophical interpretation. However we remain under the romantic spell of the previous two golden ages of our historical memory—the Periclean Age and the Mediaeval Synthesis—we are today living under the reign of pluralism and fragmentation, and this change has had infinite repercussions upon the organization of our systems of education and the role which the humanities play within them. It is no longer possible to describe the content of humanistic education as "mathematics and politics" as in the Platonic Academy, "the seven liberal arts" as in the mediaeval Cathedral school, or "the Greek and Roman classics" as at sixteenth century Oxford. Therefore even the phrase "the humanities as a unified field" has in the modern world become paradoxical and problematic.

The timetable of lectures in the Arts Course at the University of Toulouse for the year 1309, which Paetow presented in his study *The Arts Course at Mediaeval Universities,*[6] shows that except for brief treatments of works by Porphyry, Priscian, and Gilbert of Porrée, the entire four-year curriculum consisted of the logical, physical, and ethical treatises of Aristotle. And in the page from the Harvard Catalogue for the academic year 1830-31 which E. K. Rand presents as the frontispiece of his *Founders of the Middle Ages,*[7] almost the entire humanistic course of studies for the freshman and sophomore year is comprised by Livy, Homer, the Greek New Testament, Horace, Hesiod, Tacitus, Cicero, and Pliny. But in the 1967-68 catalogue of Harvard University the listing of course offerings alone comes to almost three hundred pages. Enormous expansion and proliferation of offerings characterizes the modern university. Even the smaller institutions, as well as departments of philosophy and of classics, maintain departments of art, archeology, general and comparative literature, English, German, history (in an absolutely bewildering variety of fields and areas), linguistics, music, Romance and Slavic languages. At Harvard, one interested in the humanities can also work in American Studies, South Asian Languages and Literatures, and the History of Science. At Chicago one can concentrate upon New Testament Literature, Oriental Languages and Civilizations, or the History of Culture, while Yale's offerings comprise almost every language and literature to be found on this earth including Burmese and Bulgarian. Where is now "the humanities as a unified field" in the face of these infinite riches?

We have come at last, I think, to the root perplexity of the average, committed, intellectually concerned teacher of any of the above "humanities" in any American college or university at the present time. For, although he can, in general, mark out for his discipline a glorious past, in what sense can he discern for it a unified present? In what way other than that of arbitrary or ultimately meaningless conventional placement does the division of the humanities, conceived distributively, share a commonality of method or intention? Is there, in fact, some reference to a logical kinship of explicit subject matter, some shared participation in technique, some common road of access to the realm of values, which makes the symbolic logician in the department of philosophy brother to the specialist in the Renaissance Latin lyric, or a scholar in the history of Imperial Russia from 1856-1917 akin to the computer specialist who uses his technique to establish with scientific precision the imagery of Shakespeare's problem comedies, or the specialist in the northern European painting of the fifteenth century a knowing co-worker with the Distinguished Service Professor of Structural Linguistics?

Nor is the issue only that of finding the common quality of

the humanities as a unique area of study. Equally compelling is the need to find the exact logical point of demarcation between the area of the humanities and that of the natural and social sciences. Here history is rarely more than of merely limited serviceability. For example: the distinction between the realms of fact and value has been a commonplace at least since the time of David Hume; yet there are spokesmen for the natural sciences today who tell us that "there is a likeness between the creative acts of the mind in art and in science," that "this act is the same in Leonardo, in Keats, and in Einstein," and even that "the scientific spirit is more human than the machinery of government."[8] What Hume's *Treatise* specifically asserted two hundred years ago, Bronowski's *Science and Human Values* today tacitly denies.

But the difficulties of finding a critical distinction between the humanities and the natural sciences are trivial compared to those of distinguishing convincingly between the humanistic disciplines and the social sciences. The tenets of classical humanism, its concern with moral choice, political decision, and social policy, did not permit a posture of scientific objectivity. But today there is an entire new generation of social scientists who have also forsaken Max Weber's conception of scientific *Wertfreiheit* to concern themselves with the social predicament of modern man and the possible remedies for his economic pathology and social alienation. They hold that a *relevant* social science must be present-centered and action-oriented—saturated, that is, with value preoccupations. Is this concern essentially different from that expressed in Plato's *Republic*, Aristotle's *Politics*, Cicero's *De Legibus*, or St. Thomas' *Treatise on Law*? In the sixteenth century these works would have been an integral part of a classical education in the humanist tradition. Today their analogues are the muscular texts of an applied social science. Considerations of justice and equality can no longer be excluded from studies of the distribution of world income or of the characteristic conditions of the urban environment.

If it is necessary to somehow achieve clarity about the defining properties of the humanities as opposed to the natural and the social sciences, it is equally imperative to discover a proper line of demarcation between the humanities and the fine arts. And this

presents a special difficulty because in practice it has been usual
to join them in one single complex of ultimate concern. Aesthetic
value is the preoccupation of them both, and in the clogged atmosphere of the modern multiversity with its confusion of boundaries, its quaint symbiosis of liberal and professional concerns, it
has not always been possible to maintain strict separation between
artistic creation and the historical and critical examination of its
products. Divisions of the humanities customarily contain departments of art in which courses in painting, sculpture, and basic
design alternate with those on classical archeology, mediaeval
manuscript illumination, and the tradition of easel painting in the
West, while departments of music combine courses in instrumental instruction, recital preparation, and composition with
courses in harmony, music theory, and the history of music from
the Greeks to Stockhausen. It is even possible, and sometimes
deemed especially valuable, to explore modal counterpoint in
such a way that a study of the contrapuntal techniques of the
fifteenth and sixteenth centuries is combined in the same course
with practice in writing these same styles for contemporary performance.

For this confusion there is at least some historical precedent.
Music was, of course, one of the quadrivial arts, and Boethius'
famous treatise *De Musica* (which Rand tells us was a textbook at
Oxford down into the eighteenth century) provided a basis for its
instruction. It is no help that Boethius distinguished carefully between the performer, composer, and critic of music and that he
found the first, mere slaves, the second, deficient in reason, and
only the critics, "the real musicians," since their function was
grounded in reason and philosophy.[9] What even this careful set
of distinctions cannot disguise is the essential unity of the artistic
process. It can indeed be admitted Hegelianwise that this process
has three divisions, three "moments": the act of artistic creation,
the act of artistic enjoyment, and the act of artistic judgment or
criticism; but it is doubtful if these moments can be completely
separated in the continuity of lived experience. Any artist judges
and enjoys as he paints. Any student of art history, even as he
learns the art of appreciation and the skill of criticism, is developed in his capacity of intuitive awareness as he himself engages

the problems of artistic creation. When, therefore, members of departments of art in the division of the humanities raise questions like, Is professional art education possible on university campuses? Is Design as currently defined relevant to or actually destructive of understanding of the Fine Arts? Is studio work of value to the heightening of perception and to art theory? What are the best means of relating visual studies in the arts to those in other areas of the humanities? they are asking legitimately humanistic educational questions, but in such fashion as to call into question any but the most rigid and artificial boundaries between the humanities and the arts. This too complicates our problem of definition.

Thus far I have tried to show that the definition of the humanities is rendered difficult by two things: the pluralism which results from the enormous proliferation of its component disciplines and the steady encroachment upon the area of value concern by their rivals in the field of liberal education—the natural sciences, the social sciences, and the fine arts. And this indicates that in the end we may have to modify our expectations about what we can provide in the way of an essential definition of the humanistic area. The phrase "humanistic area" is already revealing, for it suggests that even our techniques of definition are controlled by the acceptance of a guiding metaphor. The Aristotelian concept of "essential definition," of defining a class by the unique, commonly shared characteristic which is peculiar to each of its members, and by virtue of which they may be said to belong to that class, is itself founded upon a spatial, perhaps even an agrarian, image. It assumes the exhaustive divisibility of a total spatial area and of the clarity of the boundaries constituting these divisions. The logical universe of discourse mirrors the world, and the classes which it contains are fixed exclusively and exhaustively by fences which truly divide, and with no untidy segments left over. Wittgenstein has, however, suggested another model of definition, that of analogous relational properties, or, as he calls it, "family resemblances," where it cannot be said that all the faces of a family group photograph possess a single clearly recognizable feature in common, although the distribution of relational properties indicates unmistakably the single family affiliation of the component members.[10] It is a metaphor which substitutes the indefinitely characterizable entity of "the Churchill face" for the single defining characteristic of "the Hapsburg lip." For, if we assume that a series of features, such as bushy eyebrows, ruddy complexion, pointed ears, dimpled chin, blue eyes, Roman nose, sandy hair, high forehead, and the like, be taken as relational elements constituting defining characteristics, then when the family portrait is set before us, although it is obvious that each of the members belongs to the Churchill family, no single one of all these distinguishing characteristics is possessed by every face. As in the case of our practitioners of the humanities cited above— our symbolic logician, Renaissance Latin scholar, Russian historian, computer specialist for Elizabethan English, art historian, and professor of structural linguistics—it may be that a deeper analysis will reveal "family resemblances" but no single essential Aristotelian defining property, but, indeed, we must be prepared for the possibility that even this may prove chimerical.

We must also be ready to consider a third metaphor as a possible model for definition. I call it the radiation theory. It is suggested by the difficulties presented by the seemingly ineradicable overlap of value concern in the natural and social sciences, the fine arts and the humanities. It envisages not a rigid demarcation of areas, but a radiating center of intention as the defining property of any intellectual, moral, or aesthetic discipline. Unlike either the Aristotelian or the Wittgenstein models of definition, the radiation model takes as its metaphorical center neither the fixed character of an area or of a face, but the physical image of a dynamic center radiating outward like the ripples from a series of stones thrown into a pond and intermingling at their periphery with no blurring of the original sources of impetus. The overlap of classes is here a natural and expected consequence of a pluralism of intentions, and it may be, therefore, that this definitional model provides our best possible clue to the relationship between the four types of human activity which are our primary concern. In that case we must admit that the best approach to subject-matter diversity in the field of education is the radical diversity of ultimate aims.

But I want now to leave this most important issue of the

conceptual basis of definition and move on to the more prosaic matter of the logical strategy of definition as understood by logicians themselves. For it puts the task of definition which I have set for myself in this lecture within the wider framework of the past history of the humanities and of their present social function. Logicians customarily distinguish at least three kinds of definition: inferred, stipulated, persuasive. An inferred definition of the term *humanities* to be complete would have to be the product of a historical inspection of all the ways in which the term has, in fact, been used in an effort to isolate a presumed common core of meaning. But for our purposes it may be that this is not very productive, for it is possible that in the pluralism of human intentions and of cultural contexts, *there is no common core of meaning.* Then one will come up with plural definitions and their histories, and these, while historically illuminating, may actually contradict one another in spirit, if not in words, and therefore fail both theoretically and as guides to present practice.

A stipulated definition does not ask what others have meant. It stipulates "This is what *I* mean (or *we* mean) by *humanities*, and this is how *I* (or *we*) are going to use the term." And, in fact, in Public Law 89-209, establishing a National Foundation for the Arts and the Humanities, Congress has provided us just such a stipulated definition. As defined in the act, the term *humanities* includes the study of the following: "Language, both modern and classic; linguistics; literature; history; jurisprudence; philosophy; archeology; the history, criticism, theory, and practice of the arts; and those aspects of the social sciences which have humanistic content and employ humanistic methods." Unfortunately, despite this exhaustive denotative listing, Congress has not seen fit to tell us what quality or qualities these several subjects possess in common. It has failed to provide a connotative definition of the humanities. Then is this useful?

I find it very enlightening indeed. Watching how the arrows cluster, you get a sense of what must be the center of the target. There are only three places where I think it needs improvement. In the first place, to make the *practice* of the arts part of the humanities violates Congress' own procedure in setting up a National Arts Council parallel to the National Council of the

Humanities. In the second place, "those aspects of the social sciences which have humanistic content and employ humanistic methods" is obscure. It tells us nothing of what *is* humanistic content and method in the social sciences. It therefore begs the very question which Congress should have answered. But to this matter I hope in the next lecture to return.

Finally, the inclusion in the list of "jurisprudence" by itself seems ex parte pleading. I think it surely has a place in the listing, but so do "the history and ethics of medicine" in medical schools, "the history and philosophy of science and technology" in universities and engineering schools, and, for that matter, "the history and ethics of commerce" in schools of business. What is humanistic about all this, as I shall show in just a moment, is not the subject (law, medicine, divinity, technology, or commerce) but the phrase "history of" and "philosophy of."

We come then to the last form of definition, persuasive. And here one says not merely "This is what *I* mean by humanities," but rather, "This is what the term *ought to mean,* to make consistent sense out of the field customarily so designated in the colleges and universities of the western world, and I hope that it is the meaning which will prevail." In what follows I shall attempt in the briefest possible compass to present my own persuasive definition of the humanities. It is, I hope, consistent.

It is my own attempt to make sense out of the practical meaning of the humanities today. And I hope you will be persuaded by it. It makes no effort to present my articulated *philosophy* of the humanities, for this is a question of those intangible but ultimate considerations of the relation of the humanities to democracy, a free society, wisdom, vision, the realm of spirit, and the nature of man. I do indeed have ideas, feelings, convictions, on these matters too, but I shall not present them now. That is a much longer and more complicated, though no less necessary task, and I shall return to it in my concluding lecture. But it is not the task of immediate practical definition.

My *speculum mentis* begins with a very simple double dichotomy. There are the sciences and there are the arts, and each of these is in turn divided into two branches. There are the sciences of nature (including man as he is a part of nature), and there are the sciences of man as he has his own unique nonnatural culture. This is the distinction between the natural sciences and the social sciences. The arts, in turn, are divided into those concerned with the *making* of music, poetry, painting, imaginative literature, sculpture, architecture, and the like, and those concerned with the *study* and teaching of the languages, literature, history, and philosophy. This is the distinction between the fine arts and the liberal arts. The natural and social sciences, the fine and the liberal arts, exhaust the domain of mind, and it is from this beginning that I should like to draw the very simple, almost tautologous propositions which, I think, define the area of the humanities.

1. The humanities are not the natural sciences, the social sciences, or the fine arts.
2. The humanities are identical with the liberal arts.
3. The liberal arts are three, that is, the arts of communication, the arts of continuity, and the arts of criticism. (This means, respectively, the languages and literatures, history, and philosophy.)

My own definition of the liberal arts does indeed mark a break both with the mediaeval tradition and with the contemporary practice of including both the sciences and the arts in what are called "colleges of liberal arts," but its utility is great and I do not apologize for it, since it does, in my view, constitute the most reasonable approach to the contemporary role and status of the humanities. Moreover, I think it is a matter of tacit acknowledgment that the languages and literatures, history, and philosophy are, and should be, the three pillars of the humanities. Or, to change the metaphor, they are the great humanistic triptych. Which is the central panel containing the Lord depends, of course, upon who is the liberal artist and where he sits. This from Northrup Frye is both relevant and characteristic:[11] "In the study of literary scholarship the student becomes aware of an undertow carrying him away from literature. He finds that literature is the central division of the humanities [please note] flanked on one side by history and on the other by philosophy. As literature is not itself an organized structure of knowledge, the critic has to turn to the conceptual framework of the historian for events, and to that of the philosopher for ideas." Any philosopher or historian could make the same statement, placing his own specialty in the center, and flanking it with the remaining two coordinate disciplines.

Nor does anything in educational practice or in the listing of Congress seriously contradict the above scheme. True, departments of art and music are found in divisions of the humanities, but they, as humanities, will, I think, always be found to deal with the history and philosophy of art and music or with painting or music as "languages," or "literatures," that is, as communication. Where they teach musical composition or performance or painting skills, they are probably falsely placed (or at least falsely named) and should really be in music conservatories or academies of fine art.

Thus Congress's inclusion of "the history, criticism, and theory of the arts" in the humanities is valid; its inclusion of their practice is not. Archeology presents no problem; it is a part of history. But the case of linguistics (like that of logic) is more ambiguous. Practiced as a liberal art, it is (like logic) a branch of the arts of communication. Insofar as it pretends to be a science, it probably belongs among the social sciences (as relational logic conceived as mathematics probably belongs with the other branches of mathematics among the natural sciences).

There *is* a problem here, and it indicates why subject-matter disciplines need to be seen as tendencies rather than as pure specimens. Even the distinction between a science and an art probably indicates a polarity rather than a disjunction. Thus there is perhaps a humanistic tendency (subordinate and minimal as it may be) in every science, a scientific tendency (however disguised) in every liberal art.

The reason why history, for example, is so ambivalent about its own status—sometimes being housed in the division of the humanities, sometimes in the division of the social sciences, sometimes even (as at the University of Chicago) appearing simultaneously in both divisions—is because its practitioners oscillate between the impersonal search for societal laws and the consciousness that they are the custodians of group memory—those especially entrusted with the retrieval and dramatic narration of those things which it is necessary for their societies to remember. Insofar as historians stress that which allies them to the model of scientific explanation, the central importance of the *causal chain* and its predictive value, insofar as they are guided by considerations of "causal fertility" in the choice of those hypotheses which they take for investigation, they are indeed social scientists. But insofar as their criteria of "importance" in history are governed by a sense of social value, so that the narratives which they construct are not simply an "account," but an "accounting" of history, treating events as epochal or turning points in the story of the race, or for what of human significance they anticipate or reveal, then their intentions show them to be humanistic in the most authentic sense of the word.

Philosophy reveals the same ambivalence as history. Despite the somewhat misleading title of Husserl's early essay "Philosophie als strenge Wissenschaft" (philosophy as exact science) and the disingenuousness of Santayana's prefatory claim, "I am an ignorant man, almost a poet,"[12] the lure of scientific exactitude and that of poetic inspiration exert opposite influences within the philosophic tradition. The attempt to explore the structural components of human reason through the construction of a science of logic and a logic of science is one shared by Aristotle, Kant, Peirce, and the contemporary logical empiricists, although the blindness through which the latter deny philosophic competence in the areas of ethics, aesthetics, and value enquiry in general would have seemed scandalous to the former. Nor is it beside the point that Kant, immediately after having defined the role of the philosopher as that of "lawgiver of human reason" (*der Gesetzgeber der menschlichen Vernunft*) should have shifted his attention to the realm of "essential ends" (*wesentliche Zwecke*), which are "the whole vocation of man" (*die ganze Bestimmung des Menschen*) and the particular province of moral philosophy.[13] The preoccupations, even the "styles," of philosophers are patterned upon the enterprises with which they unconsciously identify. And if Carnap, Reichenbach, and their progeny seem sometimes to write with the nostalgia of scientists *manqué*, surely Plato and Nietzsche as well as Santayana have relinquished the vocation of the poet. There are as yet, I think, not many self-styled philosophers of the humanities as there are philosophers of science, but the divide between the scientific and the humanistic impulse rends the absolute unity of the arts of criticism no less than it does that of the arts of continuity.

Nor are the arts of communication immune. That human language has a music as well as a syntax, that it is emotive as well as referential, and that it serves equally as a vehicle for phantasy and for exactitude suggests contrary methodologies for literary and linguistic study. When Wallace Stevens tells us "The whole race is a poet that writes down / The eccentric propositions of its fate,"[14] implied is a total theory of language which is closer to the mythic spirit than to the scientific point of view, but when Ezra Pound produces among the inhabitants of his "Inferno" not only "the sacharescent lying in glucose, the pompous in cotton wool" but also "the obscurers of texts with philology,"[15] he parodies an impulse in the arts of communication which, out of an excessive zeal for scientific accuracy, forgets the simple immediacy of the living word. That there is such an impulse both in the teaching of the languages and literatures is clear, and it comes out both in the excessive appeal to quantitative methods and in the psychology which reduces the learning of a foreign language to the establishment of a series of conditioned reflexes apropos of verbality. The making of frequency studies whether by hand or by computer cannot be prima facie condemned—as a means it has the relative utility of the ends to which it is put—but there is often a mentality associated with it which ignores or forgets the purely instrumental character of the apparatus in its devotion to an accuracy which is more legitimately a quality of the investigations of science. Languages too may be viewed either as techniques of communication or as the foundations of experience, either as simple skills like shorthand or elementary arithmetic or as modes of perception through whose filters the world is constructed, apprehended, and transformed. The opposition between the intuitionists and the technicians infects the arts of communication no less than it does the arts of continuity and the arts of criticism.

In beginning with the fact of the enormous proliferation of the disciplines comprised under the humanities and of the slow encroachment upon their privileged area of value concern by the natural and the social sciences, I have sought to explore techniques of definition which avoid the requirement of absolute exactitude or the Aristotelian singling out of a single defining property. This has not been due to any disrespect for Aristotle, but, on the contrary, an appreciation of his insight that in our investigations we can hope for no more precision than the subject matter itself allows. And the humanities do present a complicated and a tangled challenge. In the end I have come to conclusions which are fairly conventional, and, I think, tacitly accepted, for any definition which did not attempt to understand the nature of current practice would be both idiosyncratic and of limited usefulness. My classification divides the field of the arts and sciences into four and the field of the liberal arts into three. There are the natural and the social sciences, the liberal and the fine arts; and the liberal arts (my equivalent for the humanities) are in turn divided into the arts of communication, continuity, and criticism.

But in dealing with these latter after their final identification, I have emphasized their ambiguous nature—their inclusion of the dual impulses of art and science, just as my preliminary treatment of the humanities relative to the natural and the social sciences stressed the ambiguous distinction of fact and value, and their relationship to the fine arts, that of study and creation. Art and science, fact and value, knowing and making: these are the inescapable dualisms with which we are confronted when we seek to impose order upon the multiple divisions of the intellectual life, and they give to any systematic attempt to produce clarity and precision in the defining of any set of intellectual disciplines an ineradicably dialectical character. This is a paradox which I have been able neither to avoid nor to overcome.

But it is, I believe, inherent in the very nature of the humanities as an organized—perhaps even unified—field of human endeavor, and in beginning the exploration of their contemporary relevance and the problems of intellectual and moral perplexity which they present, I have taken the task of definition as only an entering wedge—a point of initial departure upon a journey of some scope and, I hope, excitement. My guiding maxim in this definitional attempt has been throughout the brief admonition of Whitehead: "Seek simplicity—and distrust it!"

2 ❖ Values

THAT VALUE AND VALUE EXPERIENCE IS THE UNIFYING
PRINCIPLE OF THE HUMANITIES, OR, AT THE VERY LEAST, THAT THE
humanities "have to do with values," is a proposition expressing
almost universal agreement among professors of art, literature,
philosophy, and history, in the learned journals of the humanities,
and now even on Capitol Hill. The recent debate in Congress
over the appropriations to be made to the National Endowment
for the Humanities for the next fiscal year makes interesting read-
ing in this connection.[16]

"Thoughtful Americans," said Congressman Frank Thomp-
son of New Jersey, "have always recognized the importance of
these subjects which teach values, which teach judgment, which
teach appreciation for the beautiful and the permanent." Congressman Carl D. Perkins of Kentucky quoted Dr. Glen Seaborg
to the effect that "in this scientifically and technologically guided
age an overwhelming need exists for the wisdom and values that
only these human endeavors—the humanities and the arts—can
reveal to us." Congressman John R. Dellenback of Oregon was
even more explicit.

> We shall have to make some difficult judgments of value if
> we are to achieve new freedoms and avoid new—and insidious—
> forms of slavery. We shall have to strengthen our national ability
> to harness our "business" to our ideals: and to strengthen our
> ideals we shall have to strengthen the humanities. The role of the
> humanities is crucial, because they enable us to make judgments
> of value, to weigh quality as well as quantity, to ask and answer
> what it means to live well and to live with purpose. There is a play
> whose title suggests that one can learn, "How To Succeed in
> Business Without Really Trying." We all know that seldom hap-

pens. But it is certain that we shall not succeed in our ideals without really trying. How shall we try unless we support the disciplines upon which our ideals are based? We derive our notions of freedom from the humanities, our notions of justice from the humanities, our notions of compassion from the humanities. This is a practical nation; is it not practical to provide significant Federal support for the studies upon which our national understanding is based? I think it would be profoundly impractical not to do so."

Making whatever allowances you like for congressional rhetoric, it is important, I think, to consider the assumptions expressed in these comments made at a very high level of our national debate. The humanities *teach* values and judgment. They *reveal* wisdom and values. They enable us *to ask and to answer* what it means to live well. From them we *derive* our notions of freedom, justice, and compassion. Are these claims, made by the legislative champions of the humanities, ones which the practice of contemporary historians, philosophers, language teachers, and historians and critics of literature support? Or are these champions the victims of a species of humanistic cultural lag, misled not so much by what the humanities *are* in an age of democracy and science as by what they *were* in an age of aristocracy and tradition, when they sought not so much diffusion as excellence, not so much certified knowledge as intuitive wisdom? Their vision of humanistic meaning and importance is high. Do the humanities as currently practiced justify this unbounded confidence?

I do not mean to inject a note of cynicism and mistrust into a subject close to my own heart, but the ambiguities here are very real indeed, and they are only compounded by those humanists who share the ideals which Congress attributes to the humanities without finding them ingredient in present humanities practice. Even so critical an examination of the humanities as that made by William Arrowsmith finds that their failure lies in essential neglect of their valuational concerns.

> It is my belief [he says] that the humanists themselves have betrayed the humanities. Through mistaken loyalty to a cramped and academic sense of order, the humanists have turned their backs on men and expelled the native turbulence and greatness

from their studies. Thus the humanities have been distorted, and their crucial, enabling principle—the principle of personal influence and personal example—has been neglected and betrayed in a long, servile imitation of the sciences. If humanists do not have the courage to speak out for the imagination and the humanistic intelligence (which means, among other things, making intelligent statements about value), then they are not humanists at all, but merely technicians of dead and living languages.[17]

The criticism touches us where we live, and the recall to order seems admirable. But just what are "intelligent statements about value"? Edmund Wilson, perhaps our most respected literary critic in the sociological tradition, angrily telling us that the income tax should be repealed? Or Richard Popkin, perhaps our most respected younger historian of philosophy, applying what he knows about the sceptical tradition from Montaigne to Descartes to assert that the Warren Report was a poor and grossly misleading document pandering to our childish needs for security? Or Noam Chomsky, perhaps our most brilliant younger practitioner of structural linguistics, comparing America's continuing policy in Asia to that of Hitler's genocide? Is this what Arrowsmith means? Turbulence there is surely here and with God's plenty. But greatness? Imagination? The humanistic intelligence?

I am not really interested in these examples except as they indicate that there is no guarantee that talent in literary criticism, the history of philosophy, or linguistics carries with it intuitive wisdom or a privileged access to the realm of values and that Arrowsmith's phrase "intelligent statements about value" as it applies to the humanities raises infinitely more questions than it answers. Does a teacher of the humanities actually have the right to assert a preference in the field of contemporary politics and claim simply that it rests upon his study of Plutarch and Montaigne? Is he not also obligated to make clear the evidential link between his interpretation of the literary or philosophical values of the past and his political, economic, and social preferences in the present? And is there any "logic of values" which permits him to state this implicative relation in a manner which will indicate a claim upon the choices of all reasonable men? What could such a "logic of values" actually be? Or, faced with the insuperable difficulties of providing clear and irrefutable valuational evidence for specific and concrete assertions of moral, aesthetic, or social policy, is it enough for the professional in the humanities to assert the generalities of the intellectually, the morally, and the aesthetically desirable while avoiding the more compromising adventure of the reference to contemporary problems?

The question here is not so much that of making *courageous* statements of value, as Arrowsmith seems to assume, as of making *responsible* statements of value, for responsibility in axiological matters consists in the ability to show, if not a necessary, at least a highly probable link between valuational evidence and valuational judgment. And it is the difficulty of this latter which suggests to the practitioner of the humanities a more limited task founded upon a certain rational scepticism. Must the humanities "teach values" in the sense of efficiently inculcating them, or should they only identify and compare their varieties? Can we expect the humanities to put forward a single, unambiguous meaning for freedom, justice, and compassion, as Congressman Dellenback seems to assume, or is it not rather the case that close attention to these subjects as they appear in the humanistic corpus will reveal in the humanities such uncertainty, ambiguity, and confusion as to raise a real question as to whether history, philosophy, and literature produce standards or call them into question, inculcate devotion to values or introduce cynicism as to their attainment? Even if one were to shrink the compass of the humanities to the great books, to the classics of the western world from Homer to Whitehead, it would be difficult to discern a unity of value orientation. But, on the other hand, following the dialectical impulse and the oppositional strategy of a Peter Abailard, it would be easy, I think, to construct a great humanistic *Sic et Non* of the classical tradition in which we should have to include, for example, Adam Smith *and* Lenin on the value of capitalist accumulation, Aquinas *and* Voltaire on the value of the religious life, Erasmus *and* von Clausewitz (or if you prefer, Homer's *Iliad*) on the value of warfare, Tolstoy *and* James Joyce on the value of sexual loyalty.

The value record of the classics is a checkered thing, indeed, and the humanist who uses them to construct an integrated value position must be capable of finesse and a rather sophisticated selectivity. For he will find that he must be sympathetic to Hobbes' respect for the rule of law while eschewing his centralized political despotism, sensitive to the Platonic feeling for excellence without succumbing to Plato's contempt for the multitude which is its reverse side, admiring of Aristotle's preference for aristocratic magnanimity without condoning his tolerance for human slavery, approving of Rabellais' openness to the multifariousness of human experience without accepting the coarseness which seems to be its price, moved by Shakespeare's Renaissance portrayal of Roman nobility without sharing the almost physical nausea which he seems to have felt for the lower classes, siding with Rousseau's emphasis upon the virtues of natural feeling without condoning the morbid self-righteousness which is its less palatable counterpart, appreciative of Shelley's lyric gift without being committed to the human irresponsibility which was its other side, moved by Ezra Pound's espousal of the Confucian integrity without sharing in his anti-Semitic and Fascist impulses. The list of equivocal and morally ambivalent classics and classical authors is endless, and it illustrates not only the pluralism implicit in what at first glance seems to be a unified tradition, but the sense in which any integrated value conclusions which the great classical works of literature, history, and philosophy unite to form represent less what is objectively there—eternally and conclusively given and available—than what is selectively extracted or imposed upon the materials by a preexisting value configuration in the observer.

In the light of these considerations, we must examine once again the hopes of our congressional supporters that the humanities teach values and judgment, that they reveal wisdom and values, that they enable us to ask and to answer what it means to live well. And it may be that we shall be forced to supplant Congressman Dellenback's hopes that the humanities are those studies from which we derive our notions of freedom, justice, and compassion with a more modest set of expectations such as those voiced by Congressman Gerald R. Ford of Michigan. Since they add a new dimension to our discussion, I should like to quote his remarks at some length.

The reasons why support for the arts and the humanities are so essential appear daily in our newspapers. Great issues of war, of peace, of foreign policy direction confront our Nation at this time. To resolve these issues happily requires military and economic strength, to be sure. But it also requires consideration of values, of directions, of goals. It would be ironic and tragic if we forget the ends for which we fight, or if we lose sight of the ideals and sense of perspective with which the arts and the humanities provide us. The ability to think critically, to weigh and appraise evidence—in short, the lessons taught by the arts and the humanities—can help guide us in these difficult days of war.

The study of the arts and the humanities has relevance to our current domestic situation also. The members know well the issues arising from this situation: The meaning of "justice"; the relation between freedom and order; the concept of "community." The promise here is not that support of the arts and the humanities will bring a consensus on these difficult issues, but rather that study of these subjects will challenge us to remember these issues, and increase our capacity to discuss and even to differ on them reasonably rather than violently. My point is a simple one. The arts and the humanities are not frills, but are crucial to our Nation's survival and continued freedom.

Congressman Ford's remarks are interesting, I think, because in his expectations from the humanities, the notion that they are the repository of values is supplanted by the idea that they are a repository of skills—in short, the shift in expectation is from the substantive to the procedural. His demands for relevance are high: he sees the arts and the humanities as making a definite contribution to public policy, both foreign and domestic, but it is a psychological and methodological contribution rather than an axiological one. What we derive from the humanities is less a fixed ideal than a sense of perspective; above all, it is the skills of rationality: "the ability to think critically and to weigh and appraise evidence." And finally, in line with the very pluralism of value insistence and intention which we have already noted in the humanistic corpus, Congressman Ford does not expect a consensus in regard to issues of justice, freedom and order, and community, but will settle for the mere "increase in our capacity to discuss and differ reasonably rather than violently."

Two things strike one in this account of the function of the humanities. The first is that his chief demand for the skills of rationality, for the ability to think critically and to weigh and appraise evidence, is not today so much the claimed by-product of the humanities as of the sciences. Perhaps it was not always so. In the days when the trivial arts reigned and dialectic was their queen, the ability to think critically was at the heart of the human-ities, and later, after the rise of empirical science and the pressing of its claims by Bacon and his followers, the inductive require-ment was added to the deductive, and the ability to weigh and appraise evidence took its place also in a logic now more and more separated from the arts of communication and supported instead by the practical experience of the laboratory and the ob-servational disciplines. It is not, therefore, entirely by accident, but rather by a long historical process that contemporary logic with its concern with set theory and the mathematical theory of induction has become a theoretical appendage of modern science, rather than the organon which it was from the days of Aristotle through the fourteenth century, and it is no longer unnatural that when we consider the abilities to think critically and to weigh and appraise evidence, we should associate them not primarily with the humanities, but with the discipline of science.

The second thing of interest is Congressman Ford's concern with immediate relevance, with issues of domestic and foreign policy, with social issues where the meaning of justice, of the relationship between freedom and order, and of community looms large. And here, we should normally believe that what he requires is not to be found primarily in the humanities, but in the social sciences. This too is a matter of historical evolution, for topics which were once only to be treated in the classics of politi-cal and social philosophy have, as has been noted in our first lecture, found their way into the comprehensive texts of an ap-plied social science. Where once in the serious questions of social justice the fifth book of the *Nicomachean Ethics* or the ninth book of *The Republic* would have been considered relevant and il-luminating, today our mentors are rather Gunnar Myrdal, R. H. Tawney, S. G. Hobson, and John Maynard Keynes. Where once we should have looked for guidance in the relationship between freedom and order to Hobbes and Rousseau, John Locke and

Edmund Burke, Bonald, de Maistre, and John Stuart Mill, today our respected guides are the political and sociological treatises of Harold Lasswell, Seymour Martin Lipset, and C. Wright Mills. And where at a previous time we should have sought our insights into the nature of community in Plato's *Laws* and Aristotle's *Politics*, in Cicero's *De Re Publica* and Locke's *Second Treatise on Civil Government*, today we look for them in Ferdinand Tonnies' *Gemeinschaft und Gesellschaft*, the empirical studies of C. Lloyd Warner, or the utopian city planning of Paul and Percival Goodman. I am aware that Congressman Ford finds humanistic relevance less in substantive information than in procedural attitude, not so much in our knowledge as in our capacity to discuss social issues with objectivity and tolerance, but it is a serious question as to whether such objectivity and tolerance grows as easily from the warm single-mindedness of valuational commitment as from the impersonal consideration of evidence in the social science domain. We are living in an age in which the reign of the eternal verities has fallen victim to the usurpation of statistical truths, and the revolution which this displacement has accomplished has implications for the relationship between social fact and social value and for that between the humanities and the social sciences as competing claimants for a monopoly of social wisdom.

It is surely not my purpose here to aggravate the schism between the sciences and the arts, more particularly between the liberal arts or humanities and the social sciences, but the issue of humanistic value brings us back to the problem of definition which we considered in the last lecture and particularly to that piece of unfinished business to which I promised to return—what it means to refer (as the enabling act creating the National Foundation for the Arts and the Humanities did) to "those aspects of the social sciences which have humanistic content and employ humanistic methods." In making the social sciences a subject of humanistic concern, Congress already implicitly denied the sharp separation between the two areas which it would be the function of an acceptable definition to establish. Congressman Ford's remarks suggest that short of a more extreme separation of the meaning of the arts and the sciences, the distinction is extremely difficult to maintain.

Moreover, there are hints of the difficulty in a document

which preceded congressional establishment of the National Foundation for the Arts and the Humanities, and, indeed, was its chief stimulus to do so, the *Report of the Commission on the Humanities* published in 1964 under the joint auspices of the American Council of Learned Societies, the Council of Graduate Schools in the United States, and the United Chapters of Phi Beta Kappa. The statement and recommendation of that Report begins, "The humanities are the study of that which is most human. Throughout man's conscious past they have played an essential role in forming, preserving, and transforming the social, moral, and aesthetic values of every man in every age. One cannot speak of history or culture apart from the humanities. They not only record our lives; our lives are the very substance they are made of. Their subject is every man."[18]

If one takes this statement seriously, rather than ceremonially, as I propose to do, then it is clear that the overlap of concern between the humanities and the social sciences presents a practically insoluble problem. It might be argued, for example, that it is precisely man's sociality, his ability to construct and pass on his own culture which is the essence of his unique property as man, and then by the substitution of fields in the major part of the above quotation we have a counterclaim which still makes the most eminent sense. "The *social sciences* are the study of that which is most human. . . . One cannot speak of history or culture apart from the social sciences. They not only record our lives; our lives are the very substance they are made of. Their subject is every man."

But let us turn to the specific question of what is meant by the phrase "those aspects of the social sciences which have humanistic content and employ humanistic methods." What, apart from the three basic liberal arts, from the languages and literatures, philosophy, and history, could "humanistic content" possibly be? And are there any such things as distinctly and uniquely "humanistic methods" of investigation? Are the methods of science by definition nonhumanistic methods? I should certainly suppose so. Is the use of exclusively quantitative methods a humanistic method? Is the use of a computer a humanistic method? Is the use of a typewriter a humanistic method? I confess that I have the most serious doubts.

To even begin to deal with these vexed questions we need a simple set of further distinctions. We need to distinguish between (1) *subject matters,* (2) treatments of subject matter or *methods,* and (3) ultimate aims or *attitudes* in the practitioners who use these methods on these subject matters. In my opinion we shall have to maintain that there are no *intrinsically* scientific or artistic subject matters. There are only scientific or artistic *treatments* of subject matter. Thus it follows that as subject matter, such broad and general concepts as "nature" or "man" or "society" are neither exclusively scientific nor humanistic in character. Wordsworth and Newton have provided the two alternative treatments of "nature." Rembrandt and Vesalius have provided the two alternative treatments of "man." Durkheim and Balzac have provided the two alternative treatments of "society." And it follows that these differences tend to be mirrored and perpetuated in the differing treatments of professors of English literature as against professors of physics, professors of art as against professors of anatomy, professors of French literature as against professors of sociology. But this is not always the case, and when not, some of the more difficult problems begin to arise. What of the philologist who tabulates frequency lists by computer? Is this a humanistic treatment of his subject matter? And what of the economic historian who charts the development of the modern bourgeoisie merely by having his students read *Buddenbrooks, The Forsyte Saga,* and the novels of Roger Martin du Gard? Is this a scientific treatment of his? In each case the answer seems to be clearly negative. The difference between scientific and humanistic treatment seems to be finally the difference between the qualitative and the quantitative, the factual and the evaluative, the impartial and the objective, on the one hand against the purposive and the dramatic on the other. This may sound simplistic, but since I shall deal with it in greater detail in my lecture tomorrow, I need not dwell upon it now.

In any case, we do, I think, have a general idea of what is humanistic social science. We have, that is, a *denotative* knowledge. We can generally identify the specimens. Thus one would say that Garrett Mattingly's *The Armada* of ten years ago and Robert Cole's *Children of Crisis* of this year are both social science productions of a high humanistic order. Mattingly's narrative of the approach of the Armada to the British coast is as dramatic as a good novel, and his moral portraiture of the Spanish Admiral Medina-Sidonia is as brilliant as something out of Racine or Schiller. Cole's book shows a profound sympathy with his own human materials and real literary flair in expressing the dilemmas of integration in the South as it affected all strata of the population. My descriptive terms are perhaps significant. *Drama, moral portraiture, sympathy*—these are not terms found in the scientific chain of meaning, but in the humanistic complex. And in the case of Mattingly and Cole they refer to both a humanistic treatment of their subject matters and the ultimately humanistic attitude of their practitioners. This is surely what we want in our humanistically oriented social scientists, and it may just be that what we are looking for makes them mildly traitorous to the avowed ideals of their own scientific calling—that is, humanistic wolves in scientific sheep's clothing.

But I have suggested that subject-matter disciplines need to be seen as *tendencies* rather than as pure specimens and that the distinction between a science and an art probably indicates more a polarity than a disjunction. This is manifest in the sciences no less than in the liberal arts. Just as history becomes more humanistic as it moves from a logic of causal fertility to a doctrine of social importance, just as the languages and literatures become more humanistic as they move from a logic of structural features to a representation of teleology and drama, just as philosophy becomes more humanistic as it progressively uses its analytical tools for an illumination of the domain of values, so the social sciences tend to be characterized by a dual impulse, symbolized by their recognition of two distinct types of "knowing." One kind concentrates on facts and information; the other, upon understanding and awareness. One kind produces experts and technicians; the other, wise men—even social philosophers. One kind is exhausted in the network of actual social relations; the other produces an insight into the nature of social values. It is within the latter category that both Cole and Mattingly fall, and it is in terms of these divergent possibilities that we can speak of a humanistically ordered social science.

The above considerations are surely relevant to the problem

of the relation of the humanities to values, for they seem to compromise the common assumption that it is value and value experience which constitutes the unifying principle of the humanities as a body of knowledge, a program of education, and an attitude toward life. For if taken as *an exclusive claim*, it meets the opposition which we have noted in the preceding lecture. For the pure research of the natural scientist requires and inculcates the moral qualities of conscientiousness, honesty in reporting, respect for the truth, and the exciting sense of personal exploration. Bronowski has claimed that the natural scientist is as creative as the artist, and Polanyi that scientific knowledge is "personal" in all the ways to engage the moral personality.[19] And Robert Lynd and others have insisted that the social sciences have enormous utility in forming and implementing social, economic, and political value judgments. It is on this basis that Harold Lasswell has termed them *the policy sciences*.

Except for the excessive claims of Bronowski, I do not see how we can honestly deny any of this. For wherever we have activity and application, values enter in. The physician who promotes human health and the engineer who builds to facilitate human intercourse are also humanists of sorts. But then values are ubiquitous, and it is difficult to see how they can be *the* differentia, *the defining quality* of the humanities. The definitional dilemma which we face here is critical. If we wish to distinguish for practical purposes the real differences between the natural sciences, the social sciences, the humanities, and the arts, then concern with, study of, special competency in dealing with, values cannot be the *principium divisionis* of the humanities, the basis of a clear separation of them from the other disciplines. But on the other hand, if we insist, as I think that we must, that to be humanistic is to be value-oriented, then we find a continuum of humanistic concern in all the academic disciplines, and we can exclude nothing.

There is, perhaps, one way out of our dilemma. And it is to insist that although value concerns cannot be excluded from the entire range of human information, skills, and attitudes, the humanities embrace them with an earnestness that is to be found nowhere else in the spectrum of knowledge and education. When the Commission on the Humanities speaks of them as "forming, preserving, and transforming the social, moral, and aesthetic values of man in every age," when Congressman Ford asserts that "the arts and the humanities are as essential to a nation as a conscience is to an individual," behind this insistence is the idea that what the humanities contribute is a unique gift to the valuational consciousness of man. This is, I think, in no small part a direct heritage of the Roman evaluation of the pedagogical possibilities implicit in the masterpieces of Greek culture.

It is an old story (and one which Professor McKeon has surely already told) that the term *humanitas* was coined by the Romans to indicate their debt to the legacy of Greece and that this term has both an intellectual and a moral component. It signifies both "cultivation" and "moral responsibility." The latter implied in good Aristotelian fashion the acquisition of a habit, but the intellectual formulation which was the model of that habit lay in a series of much-esteemed Greek texts from Aeschylus and Sophocles to Isocrates and Plato. Thus the valuational presupposition of the humanities is a certain paradigm of the ethical life—the imitation of a model. The natural sciences may require the intellectual virtues, and the social sciences may have obvious relevance to the technical solution of extremely urgent social problems, but in neither does the moral norm play so dramatic a part as in the humanities identified not with acts of skill or application, but with the cultural conscience forged throughout the course of history. In the preceding lecture, to illustrate the mythic theory of language, I quoted the lines of Wallace Stevens: "The whole race is a poet that writes down / The eccentric propositions of its fate." These lines could be paraphrased: "The whole race through its artists sets down the model of its aspirations," and this paraphrase suggests why the humanities claim a valuational priority against the sciences, either pure or applied.

The humanities, from the Romans to the seventeenth century, were not to be separated from their pedagogical function, and this pedagogical function rested on a peculiar act of faith: faith that there is such a thing as a humanist tradition—which is nothing less than the model of what man can become—and that this tradition is constituted by the total corpus of the great works of history, literature, and philosophy. When this faith decays, the humanities sink to a lower level of relevance: they become a repository of secondary skills, or a middle-class and decorative parody of culture, or a second-hand emulation of scientific exactitude.

It is interesting, I think, that the passionate attack which William Arrowsmith has mounted against the contemporary humanities springs from a clear awareness of this background decay. For he finds them pathetically wanting in vigor—"timid, unimaginative, debased, inefficient, futile" are his adjectives—for reasons which show their incapacity to actively transmit a tradition of sturdy human value. In every field of the humanities he finds the same cult of objectivity and the same fear of valuational commitment—a cult which emphasizes facts and the accumulation of data, is obsessed with methodology and classification. And this emulation of science in the humanities has brought with it both an emphasis upon "professionalism" in the accumulation of knowledge and timidity in the face of the more old-fashioned normative responsibilities.

But the most serious failure which Arrowsmith finds in the current practitioners of the humanities is that which would have struck a mediaeval or early Renaissance moralist—it is "the gulf between one's studies and one's life, between what we read and how we live." For in the end Arrowsmith's paradigm of the teacher in the humanities is the charismatic sage. "A civilized and humanized man," he asserts, "is the only ostensive definition of the humanities—the evidence of the text we study, a living example of the meaning and value of what he teaches. What he *is* persuades or compels the student's assent to the human necessity of the text, its humanizing power. It is this man's experience that the student admires, respects, envies, tries to grasp by grasping what he believes to be its ultimate source—the work, the text, the poem, the play. He may be wrong but the impulse is natural and right. If the good teacher is not himself a great man, he has at least the stigmata of a man who would like to be great."[20] With these expectations it is not unnatural that he should find current teaching in the humanities an arid and a barren waste. "Our professors and graduate students," he concludes, "now compete only for professional plums, ever fatter professorships and fellowships. When it comes to their lives, they live as unclassically, as untouched by the humanities, as any barbarian. They are, almost all of them, the worst possible witnesses to the value of what they profess."

The charge is harsh, and it is probably excessive, for there are many dedicated teachers of the humanities whose faith in the importance of what they teach is unimpaired and who do seek to communicate an appreciation of the beauty of the texts and the relevance of the values they contain, but as an overall criticism it is sound, and it seeks to restore an emphasis upon the valuational element in humanistic instruction which has traditionally been considered its *raison d'être*.

Finally, in speaking so much about values, it is important to remember what values are. Values, although they originate in persons, affect attitudes, and qualify objects and acts, are themselves neither persons, attitudes, objects, nor acts. They are *meanings—affective-volitional meanings,* and I think it is crucially necessary to understand what this implies. As "meanings" they are concepts or ideas. As "affective" they are loci of approval or disapproval. As "volitional" they make a claim upon choice or avoidance. And this is why instruction in the humanities, if it takes its normative role seriously, cannot be restricted to the merely cognitive domain. To "teach values" may mean simply to make one acquainted with values as meanings, which is an intellectual apprehension without emotional or practical dynamic. But to "teach values" effectively would mean to communicate likewise something of the emotional quality of the feelings which attend their conceptualization and the obligation toward choice or avoidance which follows upon the "fixing" or "inculcation" of these axiological feelings. To what extent this is pedagogically possible remains a further question, and it will be to it and cognate considerations that I will address myself in my concluding lecture.

3 ✤ Knowledge

ANY ATTEMPT TO DEFINE THE DOMAIN OF THE HUMANITIES MUST BEGIN, I THINK, WITH THE BROAD DICHOTOMY BETWEEN the arts and the sciences. This was an indispensible part of the strategy of my first lecture. For it is a dichotomy which constantly reappears throughout the tradition, only to receive fixity with the nineteenth century concern with the differences between the *Naturwissenschaften* and the *Geisteswissenschaften*. But, as my second lecture seemed to indicate, this distinction has been compromised at every turn. The natural place to make the dichotomy hold—the cutting at the joints, as Plato would have said—is in the underlying distinction between "fact" and "value," but the works of Bronowski and Polanyi have raised the most serious questions about the competence of this general strategy. It will be my purpose this morning to ask rather indirectly if their insistence is to be taken seriously or if it is not the case that some sort of distinction between fact and value indeed distinguishes the sciences from the arts. In short, my problem is that of the nature of humanistic knowledge, and at the risk of apparent irrelevance I would like to approach it through a consideration of the issue raised and the enormous excitement generated by the claims of C. P. Snow almost a decade ago.

Snow's Rede Lecture of 1959, later published as *The Two Cultures and the Scientific Revolution*, fell upon sympathetic ears.[21] The soil was ripe. It told us partly what we knew uneasily without being completely willing to acknowledge, and it proposed a remedy with which we were prepared to sympathize. For the gulf between literary intellectuals and natural scientists—their mutual incomprehension, if not hostility and dislike—was patent to all.

Not the least of Snow's ingratiating characteristics was that he seemed to play no favorites. Scientists read very little, and of imaginative literature almost nothing at all. Literary people cannot distinguish "mass" from "acceleration." Scientists are apt to think a writer like Rilke to be esoteric, tangled, and dubious. Literary people believe a differential equation is a veritable witches' brew of unintelligibility and black magic. In short, is it not clear that neither the sciences nor the humanities has any monopoly upon provincialism and narrowness? At first Snow seemed to say as much. A plague upon both your houses his lecture seemed to intimate. But as we examined it more closely, even as we chuckled at Snow's sallies and applauded his wit, it became slowly clear that he was not dealing from an unmarked deck. The cards were stacked, and when they fell, it became obvious that while the sciences had erred, it was the humanities against whom the chief thrusts of his criticism were directed.

Both the camps were profoundly ignorant of one another (as Snow said, "The degree of incomprehension on both sides is the kind of joke which has gone sour"), but the cause lay in attitudes and emotions so different that the humanists and the natural scientists were simply unable to find common intellectual ground. When he tried objectively to characterize these differences of standards, assumptions, and patterns of behavior and to reduce them to their sociological base, even he was dissatisfied. Slightly more scientists are religious unbelievers. Slightly more scientists are Leftist in politics. And, as compared with the rest of the intellectual world, considerably more scientists in England (and probably also in the United States) come from poorer families. But these differences Snow was prepared to discount. For in his opinion the primary differences between humanists and natural scientists were two. In the first place scientists are naturally open-minded, progressive, oriented to change, while humanists hug the traditional culture like a blanket, are backward-looking, conservative, committed to history and the excellences which have been. In a word, the scientists "naturally have the future in their bones," while the traditional culture of the humanists "responds by wishing the future did not exist."

In the second place, scientists are readily aware of their social responsibilities, while humanists, insofar as they are aware of the human condition, view it abstractly, perhaps as personally tragic, but not as socially ameliorable. It is one thing to possess "the tragic knowledge that each of us dies alone"; it is quite another to recognize that most of our fellow human beings are undernourished and die before their time. The individual scientist, says Snow, is not so complacent before the individual tragedy that he is willing to sit back "and let the others go without a meal." On the contrary, his very sense of social responsibility causes him to view the complacency of the humanist as contemptible, and some of the humanist's literary heroes—as for example Yeats, Pound, Wyndham Lewis, and probably T. S. Eliot—as downright dangerous, as politically reactionary and ill-informed as they are socially callous and insensitive. Snow is judiciously unwilling to underwrite this charge in its entirety, but read between the lines and you will find that it commands his sympathy. The scientists, he says a little later, are more interested in the social life than most humanists; and in the moral life, "they are by and large the soundest group of intellectuals we have."

It is this last which really stings, and I must say that I do not believe that it is true. Ever since Thorstein Veblen (in his famous chapter nine of *The Theory of Business Enterprise* entitled "The Cultural Incidence of the Machine Process") tried to show that constant contact with the machine would make the modern workman precise in his intelligence, impersonal in his attitudes, and as a consequence, unpatriotic, socialistic, and irreligious in his ideology, I have been extremely suspicious of all such uncritical attempts to correlate professional aptitude and philosophy of life. Veblen was wrong, and Snow is, I think, wrong also. There may be a moral component built into the grain of science, but it is the moral of scientific method and rational objectivity which is, despite John Dewey, notoriously nontransferable to politics and the ethical life.

Snow's contention is, however, extremely revealing, for it shows that in his assessment of the two cultures, as in his novelistic intent, he is a moralist, not a dialectician, and it uncovers in the two parts of his analysis an inconsistency which takes its revenge upon him through the curiously lame proposals for reform which he implicitly advocates. On the one hand, natural scientists and humanists do not speak the same language. And on the other, humanists are hopelessly conservative and socially unconcerned. Yet it is difficult to see how Sir Charles' remedy for the first deplorable situation could possibly affect the second. A good part of his criticism is directed against the fanatical belief in educational specialization. But general education, for all its advances, has not yet learned the technique for inculcating moral virtue or social sensitivity. Granted that prospective humanists could be gotten to the stage where they could describe the Second Law of Thermodynamics—where they would not believe that Entropy was perhaps the wife of Socrates or that Yang and Lee's "contradiction of parity" was an attack upon the Eisenhower farm program—still, such relative sophistication would neither feed their impulses for social reform, nor build up the resources of their moral imagination. The difficulty with Snow is that for a moral failing he proposes an intellectual remedy, and it is one which is bound to be both irrelevant and ineffective.

But I do not wish to argue further against Snow's moral condemnation of the humanities—not because I think he is right, but because my own assessment of the problem of the two cultures lies along quite different lines. But it is necessary, I think, to point to the ambivalence (almost amounting to duplicity) which infects his treatment of the relation of the sciences and the humanities and accounts for the superficiality of his ultimate proposals for their reconciliation. For there is, indeed, something suspiciously facile about his solution; and it is definitely superficial, since it sees the difficulty (as any moralist would) in terms of human obstinacy and willfulness, rather than in that basic schism of the mind upon which this obstinacy is founded. Naturally one deplores the sharp separation of the sciences and the humanities in education. Naturally one favors a general education for men which shall propound the values of each. This is not, however, the real point. The real and infinitely more disturbing point is that when you push the superficial intent of science and the humanities back far enough, you come upon fundamentally discordant approaches to life—to a conflict of basic philosophies. Positivism is precisely that approach to the world which minimizes the importance of art, metaphysics, and literature because it bases all important knowledge upon the results and the methods of the sciences. Idealism and existentialism, on the contrary, are just those philosophies which minimize the results and the methods of science because they are all too often irrelevant to the emotional requirements of man and to the facts of his human condition.

Deep down, I surmise, Snow himself knows this, and, forced with a choice, it would, I think, be science. Here is why I think so. *The Two Cultures* seems to breathe the atmosphere of mutuality, of a magnanimity which envisages science and literature as a kind of dual monarchy jointly sovereign for men's minds and sensibilities. But in truth it does nothing of the sort. For, as we have seen, Snow charges that humanists are inordinately vain about the traditional nonscientific culture and that in the moral life it is the scientists who are the "soundest" group of intellectuals. In *The Two Cultures* reconciliation is the manifest content, but it is in his novel *The Masters* that this Dickens of the atomic age has revealed his latent message.

In this novel (as in some mediaeval morality play) science and the humanities are given their fictional personifications in the two rival candidates for the Cambridge Mastership. Jago, the Senior Tutor in English Literature, is the humanist: 50, balding and grey, a man who apologizes too much, is militantly conservative, and loves display. He has much sympathy and emotion, feels deeply, and has a passionate pride, but he is also quick-tempered, mercurial, and unstable—a man whose heart often runs away with his head. Crawford, a brilliant biologist and member of the Royal Society, is, in contrast, the scientist: a man of 56 with glossy black hair (the symbolism is of the most obvious), both cordial and impersonal, authoritative and impassive. He has a calm and steady judgment, is radical and fearless in uttering opinions, is confident, impervious, and self-assured. Whereas Jago is a more feelingful man than his rival, it is Crawford who has the broad, strong, powerful mind. The contrast between these two, Snow seems to be saying, is that between the humanities and the sciences in general, and although he places our initial sympathy on the side of the humanities, imperceptibly but forcefully this feeling is reversed, and we are in the end both relieved and convinced of its inevitable rightness when in the contest for the Mastership, the scientist finally wins. To whose strength the governance of this world rightfully belongs—this is a matter about which C. P. Snow the novelist leaves us in little doubt.

There have been in the modern world other attempts to heal the wounds of division between the sciences and the humanities— if not (as *The Two Cultures* pretends) by the delusive device of multiple sovereignty, at least by the no less misleading device of arrogating to science all the peculiar virtues of the humanities and the arts. This is the disingenuous strategy of J. Bronowski in his popular little book *Science and Human Values* to which I referred before. Bronowski argues chiefly against "the prejudice of the humanist who takes his science sourly" and who believes that science is "mechanical" and "neutral." On the contrary, he finds a profound likeness between the creative acts of the mind in art and in science and with a fine confusion refers to "those imaginative acts of understanding" which exercise the creative mind equally in both spheres. His appeal is to the act of synthesis, and he cites Coleridge's definition of beauty as "unity in variety" to show that science is "nothing else than the search to discover unity in the wild variety of nature." It is wrong, says Bronowski, to think of science as a mechanical record of facts and of the arts as remote and private fancies.[22]

So far there is much with which we may agree, and yet in the end Bronowski, for all the eloquence of his rhetoric, is unpersuasive. For he is finally forced to say that both science and the humanities express the same moral values and even that "truth" is not different in science and the arts—only more difficult to communicate in the latter. The position is equivocal, and it comes up against the stubborn facts of scientific and humanistic practice. For, undoubtedly, science *is* mechanistic in at least two respects: in its necessary reverence for "matters of fact" and in its basic reliance upon some sort of formulation of the principle of causation. On the other hand, the humanities are dramatic, emotional, and oriented to human purposes in a sense which the impersonality and objectivity of the natural sciences can never allow, and the avowed and willing anthropocentrism of the humanities is far removed from the neutral "causation" of science. The great eighteenth century philosopher Immanuel Kant treated the scientific understanding in his *Critique of Pure Reason* and the humanistic imagination in his *Critique of Judgment,* and the distinction celebrated by this separation is still, I think, eminently sound and right.

We have here, I believe, a real dualism—a distinction between the two cultures which is much more significant and disturbing than any which Snow pointed out, because it sees the age-old quarrel between the sciences and the humanities as deeply motivated, as grounded not merely in the accidents of temperament or the casual misfortunes of a narrow education, but in basic commitments founded upon a split within the structure of the human mind. Such a view of mind is uncongenial to the spirit of reconciliation (and I would not deny that there are peacemakers in epistemology as well as politics), and in its tendentiousness it runs counter to a pervasive tendency of our age. Much of contemporary philosophy, as I have shown elsewhere,[23] has been a revolt against dualism. Whitehead, Dewey, and others have tried to relax the polarities between subject and object, mind and matter, thought and emotion. But the ancient and persisting antagonism between the sciences and the humanities does, nevertheless, in my judgment, represent a real and important schism, untouched by fugitive insights that literature possesses structure and that science can be creative. Essentially the purposes of the two enterprises are different, and they are grounded respectively in the nuclear operations of the understanding and the imagination. This is the central presupposition which underlies my own approach to that polar split in the intellectual life of the whole of western society to which Snow has so provocatively called attention.

The gulf between those in the sciences and the humanities does not spring from the fact, as Snow thought, that scientists "naturally have the future in their bones," while humanists are too committed to the past to welcome the future. Nor from the belief—even if it were true—that scientists are readily aware of their social responsibilities, while humanists are profoundly uninterested in social amelioration. It springs rather from those profound original differences which separate science as a human enterprise from concern with the languages, the literatures, and the arts. For they differ in the objects to which they address themselves, the faculty of the mind which this primarily engages, and the language in which their results are expressed.

Science is the study of nature; the humanities are the study of the works of man. Science utilizes a method which adheres rigorously to the categories of the understanding; the humanities emphasize those qualities which are contributed by the imagination. Science uses a language which is impersonal, referential, objective; the humanities cultivate a language which is dramatic, emotional, and drenched with human purpose. If those in the sciences and those in the humanities do not see eye to eye, if they mistrust and misunderstand one another, and if, as Snow intimated, their attitudes are so different that "even on the level of emotions, they cannot find much common ground," this is hardly surprising. They look at different aspects of our world. In a most important sense, they *think* differently. And quite literally, they speak two separate languages.

It is hard to see how it could be otherwise. Or even why it should be. The physician and the photographer, the jurist and the engineer, also speak separate languages. It is a presupposition of professionalism—of that division of labor which characterizes the duties of civilized men no less than the multiple possibilities of the intellectual life. But I agree that the difference between the humanities and the sciences is a privileged case—a more profound and universal case, precisely because it is founded upon the structure of the human mind, because it expresses diametrically opposed cognitive needs of the human person.

Except for Kant, it is perhaps Santayana who locates our difficulty most accurately, who sees that the basic problem of the conflict between the sciences and the humanities arises at the intersection of the understanding and the imagination.

> We have, [he says] memory and we have certain powers of synthesis, abstraction, reproduction, invention—in a word, we have understanding. But this faculty of understanding has hardly begun its task of deciphering the hieroglyphics of sense and framing an idea of reality, when it is crossed by another faculty—the imagination. Perceptions do not remain in the mind, as would be

suggested by the trite simile of the seal and the wax, passive and changeless, until time wears off their sharp edges and makes them fade. No, perceptions fall into the brain rather as seeds into a furrowed field or even as sparks into a keg of powder. Each image breeds a hundred more. The mind, exercised by its own fertility and flooded by its inner lights, has infinite trouble to keep a true reckoning of its outward perceptions. It turns from the frigid problems of observation to its own visions; it forgets to watch the courses of what should be its pilot stars. Indeed, were it not for the power of convention in which, by a sort of mutual cancellation of errors, the more practical and normal conceptions are enshrined, the imagination would carry men wholly away,—the best men first and the vulgar after them.[24]

Santayana's assessment of the power of the imagination is perhaps extreme—it is the estimate of a highly imaginative man —but this picture of the twin endowment of the human mind is surely relevant to the problem of the two cultures. For it is upon the understanding with its factuality—its work, as Santayana says, of "deciphering the hieroglyphics of sense"—that physics, chemistry, biology, and the other natural sciences take their foundation; and it is upon the imagination and its fertility—its dependence upon fantasy and myth—that literature, art, metaphysics, and the other humanities take their stand; and each claims validity for its own interpretive picture, its own vision of the world.

There are, then, not one, but two "maps of reality"—one sober, factual, claiming to be custodian of the literal truth, the other mythical, playful, but claiming to point the way to a deeper wisdom—which compete for allegiance in the institutional framework of the modern university as they do in the divided mind of every individual man. What wonder, then, that there should be two cultures giving emotional partisanship as well as sociological embodiment to these two cognitive needs?

It is surely no secret that these needs are in serious opposition. For to call the understanding "factual" and the imagination "playful" is but to state in other language what we all recognize as the difference between objectivity and subjectivity—the neutral claims of an externalized nature versus the internal claims of human purposes. Wallace Stevens, one of the most brilliant of contemporary poets, not long dead, has spoken of poetry thus: "It is a violence from within that protects us from a violence from without. It is the imagination pressing back against the pressure of reality. It seems, in the last analysis, to have something to do with our self-preservation; and that, no doubt, is why the expression of it, the sound of its words, helps us to live our lives."[25]

Stevens' image of "the imagination pressing back against the pressure of reality" is valuable, because it serves again to set the functioning of the imagination and the humanities against that of the understanding and the sciences. The understanding gives way before the pressure of reality; indeed, it is itself a kind of cognitive "reality principle" which deals with the world on the world's own terms. And it is not accidental that Freud, who originated this terminology, countered this activity by that of the pleasure principle, which, often thwarted at the level of overt activity, expresses itself in the substitute gratification of unrestrained fantasy. The imagination is the center of the life of fantasy, and, whether in literature, in myth, in poetry, in religion, or in art, it presses back against reality with all the force and energy of its own subjective claims.

When in 1605 Sir Francis Bacon published his *Advancement of Learning*, included in the "Survey of Learning," which comprised his second book, was also a consideration of poetry. The world, says Bacon, is inferior to the soul of man in magnitude, rarity, variety, and goodness. And since it appears that poetry serves to promote magnanimity, morality, and delectation, "therefore it was ever thought to have some participation of divineness, because it doth raise and erect the mind by submitting the shows of things to the desires of the mind; whereas reason doth buckle and bow the mind unto the nature of things."[26] Bacon's *Advancement of Learning* and my quotation from Wallace Stevens have more than three hundred years between them, but they both presuppose an understanding (Bacon calls it "reason") which "doth buckle and bow the mind unto the nature of things." And when Stevens speaks of the fantasy "pressing back against the pressure of reality" and Bacon of poetry as elevating the mind "by submitting the shows of things to the desires of the mind," both are describing the purposive imagination upon which the humanities are based.

To assert, as I have done, that the problem of the two cultures is ultimately the problem of the understanding and the imagination is to localize it in the constitution of the human mind. But clearly this has further implications for the separate languages which the natural sciences and the humanities speak. For if the human understanding is the source of natural science as the imagination is the source of the humanities, each of these faculties of the mind is uniquely responsible for its own table of categories, its own alphabet of forms, its own vocabulary of concepts, its own family of meanings, and these categories and meanings, alphabets and vocabularies, seem to be in profound opposition to one another.

We have here, I think, something like one of those instances of which Gilbert Ryle, the Waynflete Professor of Metaphysical Philosophy at Oxford has treated in his Tarner Lectures at Cambridge in 1953 which he entitled *Dilemmas*.

> There often arise [he says] quarrels between theories, or, more generally, between lines of thought, which are not rival solutions of the same problem, but rather solutions or would-be solutions of different problems, and which, none the less, seem to be irreconcilable with one another. A thinker who adopts one of them seems to be logically committed to rejecting the other, despite the fact that the inquiries from which the theories issued had, from the beginning, widely divergent goals.[27]

The relevance of this formulation to the problem of the two cultures is, I think, clear, for its suggests the uneasy mutual confrontation of the language of the understanding and that of the imagination. In terms like *true and false propositions, error, scientific law, causality, chance, prediction, fact, equilibrium,* and *stasis,* we have a series of concepts in what I will call "the scientific chain of meaning." In terms like *appearance and reality, illusion, destiny, free will, fortune, fate, drama, happiness, tragedy,* and *peace,* we have a series of concepts in what I will call "the humanistic complex." And the confrontation of these two provides an excellent illustration of what Ryle has spoken of as quarrels between different lines of thought which are not necessarily rival solutions of the same problem, but address themselves to different problems: indeed, as I have suggested, to different needs of our cognitive situation.

There is an obvious and crucial difference between the language of the understanding and the language of the imagination, and yet there is also a paradoxical similarity between them. Where the scientist is concerned with the truth and falsity of propositions, the poet is concerned with the appearances and realities of the world, and so the problem which the one deals with under the rubric of "error" the other must consider under the heading of "illusion." Both Einstein and Cervantes are concerned with the nature of "relativity," but scientifically the problem of the tensor calculus is what its application will yield in errors of physical measurement, while the poetic problem of the mind of Don Quixote is just the natural history of those illusions which stem from the inability to distinguish fact from fiction. And so throughout our list. The blinding of the unhappy Oedipus is not a matter of "prediction" but of "fate," while, conversely, the incidence of blindness among the newborn to a medical statistician is not a matter of "fate" but of "prediction." The mathematician's account of the continual casting of the dice makes reference to the scientific notion of "chance," but the act by which Desdemona loses her handkerchief to Iago is not an act of "chance" but of "misfortune." And yet, such is the supposedly contradictory character of the scientific chain of meaning and the humanistic complex that positivists in philosophy like Reichenbach and Carnap will insist that to speak of "appearance and reality" is nonsense, and poets like T. S. Eliot and Wallace Stevens will complain that in a world dominated by the ideology of mechanistic causation, real "tragedy" is no longer possible.

But my concern here is less with the alleged conflict between specific concepts like "error" and "illusion" or "destiny" and "scientific law" than with the general contrast presented by the language of the understanding and the language of the imagination upon which the humanities rest. And the meaning of this contrast can be easily seen if we ask what is the common quality which they respectively illustrate. What is the generic property of terms like *illusion, destiny, fate,* and *tragedy,* and how does this differ from the generic property of terms like *error, causality, prediction,* and *fact?* If we consider the question in the light of its historical occurrence, we may at first be tempted to answer it in the now-famous terms of Ogden and Richard's classic distinction, and to say that the language of the understanding is referential while that of the imagination is emotive. But closer examination will, I think, convince us that this distinction, although not false, is insufficient. It is plausible, but it persuades us to be satisfied with a property rather than an essential attribute, and hence, manages to conceal what is really there.

The essential characteristic of the terms of the scientific chain of meaning is not that they are referential, but rather that what makes their reference possible is objectivity and factuality. And the essential characteristic of the terms of the humanistic complex is not that they are emotive, but that such emotivity as they possess is due to their function as vehicles for the expression of purposiveness and drama. The natural sciences, for all that they are undeniably a human enterprise, are a tribute to man's ability to expurgate all mythical, teleological, and anthropomorphic elements from his thinking. They illustrate his interest in factuality. They show him at the utmost limit of his objectivity. The humanities, for all that they employ a logic and require a structure of their own, are a demonstration that drama, purposiveness, and self-concern are inescapable and indispensible elements of the human situation and the expressiveness which it requires. They illustrate man's dramatic instinct. They show in its most elegant form the propensity for teleological interpretation in man.

This, as I have said, is a real dualism—a clear split down the center of the intellectual life, and it is difficult to see how, with such diametrically opposed cognitive needs, it could be otherwise. But as we have seen from the first lecture, this does not mean that there is no commerce between the two rival territories and that the sometimes vague boundary which separates them is not crossed. It is possible to be a "raw empiricist" in the humanities, to employ in the languages and literatures, history, and philosophy a narrowly analytical methodology. And as Arrowsmith and others have pointed out, the method of scientific analysis when applied to the humanities has sometimes unfortunately produced a mentality which is less fitted to creatively continue a vital human tradition than to peep and botanize upon its grave.

The distinction between the understanding and the imagination which I have drawn, and its utility as a basis for separating the sciences and the arts, also has implications for the problem of values, and it perhaps explains our natural urge to find that "value" and "value experience" are the unifying principles of the humanities. For, although in a broader sense it is surely true that the objectivity and factuality of science are values, both in their predictive consequences and in their reference to the narrowly cognitive functions of the human mind, they do not touch the heart of purely human subjectivity and feeling. We can sympathize with Santayana when he scorns science precisely because its lack of emotion, its objectivity, denies the very quality which distinguishes the human person from the lens of a microscope. "There is nothing worth having in kingship," says one of the characters in his *Dialogues in Limbo,* "but what a penniless dreamer may enjoy in conceiving it, and the illusion in love, in wisdom, and in enthusiasm is the true and only virtue in them. To have a clean and scentless intellect, my noble Democritus, that should merely report things as they are, would be almost like not existing; so clear and transparent a medium would hardly be a soul."[28]

The self which Kant talks about in the *Critique of Pure Reason* is precisely the clear and transparent ego of the scientific observer, hardly to be distinguished from the lens of a scientific instrument, but the self implied by the *Critique of Practical Reason* and the *Critique of Judgment* is indeed a soul—a human self capable of a recondite taste and haunted by the sense of moral obligation. Without an intuition of form and organic unity which is the basis of all taste and all aesthetic judgment, without the insistent claims of moral obligation which gives life its peculiarly social flavor and consolidates all institutional bonds, the humanities are unthinkable.

Humanistic study includes the literary masterpieces which illuminate the relations between appearance and reality, portray the operations of fortune and fate, and dwell upon the factors of drama and tragedy in human life. It includes the historical efforts to reveal the factors of destiny and fortune as they qualify the continuity of political tradition and give to group memory its qualities of relevance and significance. It includes the philosophical attempts to place man within the dimensions of his cosmos so that his destiny, his tragedy, his happiness, and his peace are defined within the limits of the universe he inhabits, bounded by transcendence on one horizen and brute nature on the other. These are the areas of significant values and value experiences, and it is not the part of exaggeration and arrogance, but of simple truth, to say that the essential task of the humanities is to function as their custodian.

4 ✳ Culture

My first three lectures on the problems of definition, values, and humanistic knowledge have been, in a sense, theoretical. They have done what was in my power to do in the way of analyzing the meaning and the functioning of the humanities as a body of knowledge and as ingredients in the educational process. And my lecture tomorrow on ultimate aims will return to this same theoretical concern. But today I want to consider certain difficulties which the humanities face as a consequence of their historical evolution, and as beset with the general dangers of our current cultural situation. My concern will largely be with matters which Whitehead in *Adventures of Ideas* would have called "sociological." I know no better way to begin than with the opening paragraph of a short essay entitled "The Crisis of the Mind" written by Paul Valéry just after the First World War. That was a long time ago—1919—but the words were prophetic.

> We later civilizations, we too know that we are mortal. We had long heard tell of whole worlds that had vanished, of empires sunk without a trace, gone down with all their men and all their machines into the unexplorable depths of the centuries, with their gods and their laws, their academies and their sciences, pure and applied, their grammars and their dictionaries, their classics, their romantics, and their symbolists, their critics and the critics of their critics. . . . We were aware that the visible earth is made of ashes, and that ashes signify something. Through the obscure depths of history we could make out the phantoms of great ships laden with riches and intellect; we could not count them. But the disasters that had sent them down were, after all, none of our affair.
>
> Elam, Nineveh, Babylon were but beautiful vague names, and the total ruin of those worlds had as little significance for us

as their very existence. But France, England, Russia . . . these too would be beautiful names. *Lusitania*, too, is a beautiful name. And we see now that the abyss of history is deep enough to hold us all. We are aware that a civilization has the same fragility as a life. The circumstances that could send the works of Keats and Baudelaire to join the works of Menander are no longer inconceivable; they are in the newspapers.[29]

Some of the current pessimism which infects the humanities is predicated upon the same sense of mortality and impending catastrophe as informs these words of Valéry—grows out of a tragic recognition that the abyss of history is deep enough to hold us all, that our civilization is fragile enough to be destroyed by a wrong decision in the White House or the actions of a Kremlin dictator who has lost his sense of balance. The circumstances that could send the works of Proust and Picasso, of Joyce and Stravinsky, to join the works of Menander are no longer inconceivable; they are in the daily newspapers!

What can be the fate of the arts in an era that is actually conscious "that a civilization has the same fragility as a life," when the meaning of the arts rests upon the security that although the individual life is short, the fruits of its creation may permanently endure and secure for the individual his special objective immortality in time? The question suggests a contradiction in terms. The meaning of art is the assertion of life and the struggle against nothingness. The interior problem of the artist—no matter how he chooses to sublimate or dissemble it—is the problem of his own death. And he solves this problem by inserting into the world of culture those spiritual fragments—novel, painting, or symphony—through which he hopes to live on after his body is but dust. The misery of Van Gogh belongs to artistic theodicy only if the flaming countryside of the Arles canvasses persists on the walls of the Orangerie or at the Hague. The deafness of Beethoven has point only if the A Minor Quartet which is its fruit is a potential spiritual education for every remaining ear which cares to listen. Every artist makes his peace with his individual death, but only on condition that culture remains alive. To make art in full awareness that there may be no future is as essentially aimless as the concentration of the absent-minded professor who types for hours, unconscious that there is no paper in the machine on which he writes.

There is, of course, a reasonable objection to this line of reasoning. For it has not distinguished between the creative arts, which always signify our acknowledgement of the claims of the future, and the humanities proper, which are studies, not creative acts, which form tradition rather than adventure, and which, therefore, by their very nature as traditional materials require us to look backward, to be attentive not to future but to past. The objection is attractive, not least because it implies one possible response for a world possibly drifting toward a dreadful destruction. If you had asked a Roman nobleman living in the last despairing days of the Roman Empire for what he had to live, he might well have replied: "For the future—nothing. But I remember my Horace and my Virgil, my Catullus and my Caesar, and in them and through memory, I recreate the grandeur that was Rome, and in this I find the meaning of my life. History and tradition and memory are the vehicles through which the humanities will always serve their proper function."

But there is something faulty in this point of view also. For to look to the past for its own sake is a confession of the meaninglessness of the present, and the focus of humanistic concern was never rightfully the denial of the present, but the addition of ancient resources for its enrichment. Yet obsessive backward-looking has always been a danger. From the fifteenth to the seventeenth centuries was the great age of the humanities, but even in their prime they were afflicted with the dangers which come from only looking backward. At its best, this means recovery and conservation; at its worst, pedantry and failure of nerve. The principal function of Renaissance scholarship was to deny the thrust of five hundred years of Christian Scholasticism in order to provide a Graeco-Roman base for the newer secular culture. This was the avowed progressive intention of humanists from Petrarch to Erasmus. But in centuries following, the claims of the humanities were advanced by men like Estienne, Casaubon, and Scaliger—scholars rather than moralists—for whom the emendation and rectification of the texts had become even more important than a perusal of the wisdom they contained. And this was not only pedantry, it was also a betrayal of the impulse from which the humanistic studies had sprung.

The humanities are an invention of the Romans, and the Greek classics which composed them were supposed not only to cultivate the mind but to humanize practice. Pedantry can do what it may to suppress the element of practice, but when the humanities are effective as a cultural force, they may be expected to have their influence upon society in general, even upon politics. For example, nineteenth century education in the humanities was a success to the extent that it provided leaders whose humanist culture was not irrelevant to their political effectiveness. Guizot and Macaulay are cases in point, and even Bismarck is inseparable from the culture of post-Napoleonic Goettingen.

But from this original emphasis of the humanities upon practice there arises a possible danger, and we should therefore inquire candidly in what sort of moral service the humanities have been enlisted. And when we do so, we shall, I think, inevitably discover that their historic use has bequeathed to the reception of the humanities today certain inevitable difficulties. The humanities almost by original definition deal with those cultural products in which are demonstrated what it means to be essentially "human." And this demands not merely a philological skill but is grafted upon a set of attitudes reflecting the dominant ideals which informed the best thought at the time when the humanities flourished. And in the fifteenth, sixteenth, and seventeenth centuries this means an unwavering bias in favor of *aristocracy*.

At this point the problem of the humanities becomes an integral part of the problems of historical sociology. Renaissance humanism was intimately connected with Renaissance education. Renaissance education was both aristocratic and highly individualistic. The individualism was in part a reaction against the supposed intellectual unity of the Middle Ages, but the aristocracy was simply a perpetuation of the baronial side of the feudal tradition. Socially and economically, both Renaissance education and Renaissance humanism were maintained under a pyramidal class structure. Unfortunately, this very fact serves to call into question the permanent worth of the values which early humanism nurtured and developed.

Aristocratic values are of course beyond question in an aristocratic society, but in a social order nominally democratic, the right of personal cultivation must not be limited to a small segment of the population. The connoisseur spirit, which has all too often been associated with the humanist tradition, has little place in a democratic society, and it may be this consciousness, lurking in the background, which in the scheme of modern education has placed the humanities at a disadvantage compared with the natural and the social sciences. For whatever the place of *litterae humaniores* (humane letters) in some Platonic utopia, to an actually existing democratic society faced with the dual threats of economic stagnation and political extinction, they often seem but a kind of luxury which it finds itself ill able to afford.

Aristocracy is a tendency at the very heart of the humanistic tradition and from the Greeks to the nineteenth century permeates it. Jebb and Jowett, no less than Plato and Cicero, were aristocrats in spirit. But if this is one of the unconscious stumbling blocks to present acceptance of the humanities, another is the way in which almost from the beginning they have been used to implement values which were more narrowly nationalistic than universal. And this represents a split within the ranks of the humanists from the sixteenth century onward. The broader interpretation is represented by Erasmus; citizen of the world, committed to no city and no country, writing an elegant Latin as if to demonstrate the promise of his universalism and speaking in the name of excellence and moderation to the entire European community of reasonable men. The narrower interpretation is represented by Montaigne, patriot of France, citizen of Bordeaux, and loyal subject of the king, who writes in his beloved French as if to certify the more provincial flavor of a humanism which, however founded upon Greek skepticism and Roman stoicism, is Gallic to the core. Unfortunately, it is the spirit of Montaigne rather than that of Erasmus which has most often carried the day.

All too often in the emerging nationalism of the modern world where the tradition of the humanities has been strong, it has been used in the service of interests which are local and selfish. A chauvinistic people's conception of the humanities is of something which will endorse its morality and flatter its patriotism. Just so nineteenth century Prussia used the conception of the Roman Empire. So Mussolini discovered that Dante was a Fascist. So the Russians have found that Tolstoy was a theorist of the class struggle. So the Germans had little difficulty in converting Schiller into a Nazi hero. This in itself is not surprising. But what is more disturbingly to the point is that to a large extent scholars in the humanities have themselves contributed to the provincializing of the tradition. Long before totalitarianism was a word, Germans looked with suspicion upon the foreigner who dared write a life of Goethe, French philosophers were convinced that before one could understand Descartes one must be a French philosopher, and Dante scholarship was a jealously guarded Italian enterprise. To the extent that this was the case, the humanities had already failed in their social function. For they had forced into a narrow and distorted perspective what was in reality world literature and the heritage of all of western culture.

I have used the phrases "world literature" and "western culture" as if their meaning was obvious, their import self-evident, their relevance to our judgments of the humanities a certitude. But this very obviousness shows something about the frame of reference of a modern culture infected with pluralism and with the fact of conflict ever before its eyes, yet looking backward nostalgically to those moments when life was simpler, men were held together by a common theology and ethics (if not by a common political aspiration), and the fund of literary and artistic riches was sufficiently limited to be educationally manageable.

Thirty years ago Robert Hutchins and Mortimer Adler at the University of Chicago, in an effort to decree a unity which in fact was not to be discerned in the society in which they lived, limited by fiat the indispensable cultural baggage of western man to 107 "great books" beginning with Homer and ending with Sigmund Freud. It is instructive to compare the critical reaction to this proposal then and now. The first responses reflected dismay at the number and heterogeneity of the works included. How in a mere four-year period could one possibly do justice to 100 books as rich and as demanding as Plato's *Republic*, Dante's *Divine Comedy*, Gibbon's *Decline and Fall of the Roman Empire*, Dostoievsky's *The Brothers Karamazov*, Russell and White-

head's *Principia Mathematica?* Above all, where would one find
those polymaths—learned in the entire spectrum of the arts and
sciences—who could instruct with equal competence whether the
materials were Euclidean geometry, ancient Greek history, the
mediaeval epic, Renaissance physics, baroque drama, the nineteenth century novel, or contemporary psychoanalytic theory?

The trouble with this cultural baggage was that it was too
heavy a load to carry, and those who adopted the program even
in the best of faith, found it necessary to slowly cut, diminish,
excise, select, eliminate, subtract, and summarize—in short to
throw overboard—until the weight grew manageable. But at this
point the program could more justly have been called not the
"great books," but the "great pamphlets" of the western world;
something like the *Summa Theologica* of St. Thomas Aquinas cut
to fit the requirements of *The Reader's Digest!*

Today, thirty years later, the tide of criticism has turned—in
fact, it has almost completely reversed itself. The trouble now lies
not in the weight, but in the lightness—in the provincialism of the
phrase *"western* culture" in a world where Katanga is more important than Canterbury, Laos than Los Angeles, Vietnam than
Vienna. Where in our humanities curriculum is the Egyptian
Book of the Dead, the Confucian *Analects*, the Icelandic Sagas,
the *Baghavad-Gita*, the astronomy of Al Farabi, the novels of the
Lady Murasaki, the collected folktales of the Watrubi and the
Maiori? The Hutchens and Adler list, we now see, contains not
too many items, but too few. Culture has outrun the European
heartland to encompass the world.

Thus our concept of the humanities slowly changes, slowly
enlarges, and with this enlargement come new tasks hitherto un-
dreamed of. When the chief content of the humanities was the
literature of Greece and Rome, it was possible to educate a gentleman according to the canons of Cicero and Quintillian, and the
basic humanist skills of analysis and appreciation were relevant to
problems set by a limited political universe. Education in the
humanities was then an education in values narrowly limited by a
sense of classical importance and by a concept of culture which
had been formed upon the model of the sharp distinctions between Greeks and barbarians, Romans and Asians, Christians

and pagans. To this important, but limited, task have now been added others.

I do not wish to repeat what I am sure that Professor Mc-Keon has already clearly stated. The world today is torn by many conflicts—political, ideological, cultural. How are they to be adjudicated? When the humanities are used as agencies of propaganda, the answer is stated dogmatically, in advance, and nations try desperately, and in some cases shamelessly, to extract from the tradition of humane letters some shallow justification of the exclusive rightness of their own political course and cultural prejudices. But when, on the other hand, the humanities are granted that impersonality and universality which rightly finds its source in the qualities of a humane imagination, then one of their functions is a profound study of the humanistic expressions of the many cultures of the world in the hope that such study will reveal a common core of humanity without fear of a hopeless relativising of human values. This is the final triumph of cosmopolitanism over the provincial outlook.

A world of difficulty is expressed in the opposition of these two terms, *cosmopolitanism* and *provincialism*. And at bottom it is probably the root issue behind most of the crucial questions which collectively might be termed the present crisis of the humanities. In one sense, as I have indicated, the spirit of universalism has always been expressed by humanistic thought at its best, has never been completely lost in the humanistic tradition. The literatures of Greece and Rome, precisely because they were a common property, could be a force permanently struggling against an obsessive nationalism. And the Greek and Latin languages, precisely because they were dead languages, could serve as a fund of meanings—common in their relevance—which could operate against the too limited and local flavor of the vernacular tongues as they emerged from early mediaeval Europe. And it is therefore characteristic that "humanism" as a concept is inseparable from the successive waves of universal influence which have swept over the continent of Europe: Renaissance, classicism, Enlightenment, romanticism, and the rest. But the cosmopolitanism which is characteristic of the contemporary world is so all-encompassing, so inclusive of areas of the world previously ignored, that it makes terms like *Renaissance* and *Enlightenment* seem almost narrow and provincial; as meaningless to a contemporary inhabitant of Liberia or Peking as to a man from Mars.

It may seem that when the opposition between provincialism and cosmopolitanism is posed, the mind naturally tends to shrink from the narrowness of the former and to embrace the greater amplitude of the latter. But this cosmopolitanism to which we so naturally tend, and which is the prevailing temper of the modern world whether we like it or not, has its own peculiar dangers, above all for the creative arts, but also for the vitality of the humanities as a living part of culture.

We are in the presence here of a difference between cultural youthfulness and cultural old age, a distinction first put forward by Nietzsche and afterwards vividly exploited by Spengler. However uncomfortable we may feel in the presence of these thinkers, their insight is to be taken seriously. Both were aware that to be in either stage of culture means to pay a certain price. A youthful culture is naive, fanatical, mythic, narrow, provincial, firm, and dogmatic in its beliefs, but infinitely creative in its artistic self-expression. A culture growing old is tired, tolerant, sophisticated, broad, cosmopolitan, pluralistic in the sources from which it draws, but intellectual and derivative rather than fresh and intuitive in its cultural self-expression. It is the difference, as both expressed it, between a Homeric and an Alexandrian age.

For an artist living in an Alexandrian age the problems are acute. Either he abandons the narrow western tradition for which the entire previous history of his craft has fitted him and espouses the rootless pluralism of the age, or, adhering to the outlook of the past, he senses that he is old-fashioned, an anachronism in his own time.

A living artistic tradition depends upon myths. By myths I mean the stories which a people tells itself to unfold the meaning of its life. These stories are not merely encapsulated in the greatest products of painting and literature, they also form the basis of the tales told to children for their entertainment and instruction. But in a cosmopolitan age these stories are no longer recited with conviction as our forefathers recited the parables of the Old Testament, or as even so scientific a historian as Thucydides gave credence to the factuality of the Trojan War. For when belief in the stories fails in the common consciousness, then their appearance in the literary media is merely nominal, and their treatment becomes deeply ironic—the tongue-in-cheek response of a sophisticated skepticism.

The ancient Greek drama was predicated upon the deeply felt meaningfulness of the stories which grew up around the Trojan War and the fate of the house of Atreus. The modern French drama draws almost obsessively upon the same theme. But in the mouths of Gide and Giraudoux, of Anouilh and Cocteau, these stories are all inherently ironic, inverting their original naiveté to make some completely contemporary point, Freudian or existentialist as the case may be, but in the skeptical Gallic idiom which is the very antithesis of Aeschylus or Sophocles and which would have been an impossibility before the appearance of Descartes and Voltaire.

The characteristic pattern of the arts in an Alexandrian culture is an eclecticism or amalgam of traditions, tolerant of all, blurring the primitive roots by which the stories were originally anchored in lived experience. Its resources are, therefore, multiple but aimless, themes chosen rather than given, and chosen from an arsenal which contains not merely the epic of the Greeks, but the Chinese novel, the Hindu erotic story, the Arabic Hadith, and the African folktale. The riches of world culture are available for appropriation, but rather as the exhibits are laid out in a museum, the product of classification rather than direct experience, an exercise in pedantry rather than creation.

Already a hundred years ago, Nietzsche said it well.

> Our art reveals this universal trouble: in vain does one depend intuitively on all the great productive periods and natures, in vain does one accumulate the entire "world-literature" around modern man for his comfort, in vain does one place one's self in the midst of the art-styles and artists of all ages, so that one may give names to them as Adam did the beasts: one still continues eternally hungry, the "critic" without joy and energy, the Alexandrian man, who is at bottom a librarian and corrector of proofs, and who, pitiable wretch, goes blind from the dusty books and printer's errors.[30]

Nietzsche is, as usual, histrionic and extreme, but in his concern for the fate of the arts in a cosmopolitan age, he at the same time tells us unconsciously something of the fate of the humanities as well. It is almost as if the healthiness of the arts follows an inverse law, as if they are subject to a permanent and natural dilemma of cosmopolitanism. If a culture is provincial, its outlook will be narrow and fanatical, but its arts will flourish. If a culture is cosmopolitan, its attitude will be broad and tolerant, but its arts will suffer from the very character of its pluralism and skepticism. In one sense the eclipse of the arts may be a boon to the humanities, for, as Nietzsche said, it pushes to the forefront just those techniques of emendation, classification, and criticism upon which the humanistic tradition has thrived. But in a larger sense, to see it so would be false consolation indeed. For the issue here is basically that of an impoverishment of the mythical consciousness, and this seems certain to have its unfortunate repercussions on the humanities as well as the arts. For the humanities, like the arts, as I tried to indicate yesterday, are the products of the imagination, and it is only myth that saves us from the excessive claims of the understanding and frees the powers of the imagination for their proper task.

> Let us now think [says Nietzsche once more] of the abstract man unguided by myth, the abstract education, the abstract morality, the abstract justice, the abstract state: let us picture to ourselves the lawless roving of the artistic imagination unchecked by native myth: let us imagine a culture which has no fixed and sacred primitive seat, but is doomed to exhaust all its possibilities, and to nourish itself wretchedly on all other cultures—there we have the present, the result of Socratism, which is bent on the destruction of myth. And now the mythless man remains eternally hungering amid the past, and digs and grubs for roots, though he has to dig for them even among the remotest antiquities. The terrible historical need of our unsatisfied modern culture, the assembling around one of countless other cultures, the consuming desire for knowledge; what does all this point to, if not to the loss of myth, the loss of the mythical home, the mythical maternal bosom?[31]

It is interesting to see that Nietzsche not only diagnoses the disease, but uncovers its etiology. The destruction of myth is due to what he calls Socratism, and what he means by Socratism is nothing else than the theoretical posture, the unrelenting rationalism of science. This rationalism has two facets: one theoretical, the other pragmatic. Science enthrones the concept of literal truth; it operates its logic of discovery and explanation with an eye to removing the veils from nature, but by so doing, it at the same time makes nature subservient to the satisfaction of man's needs or at least of what he conceives his needs to be. From the isolation of the laboratory and the cubicles of the mathematical calculators comes the public forum of applied research and the massive workshops of a socialized technology. All this slowly permeates the domain of the public consciousness, revising its ideals and infecting its notions about the meaning of human life. So that at last the perspective of the philosopher with his yearning after the complex accuracy needed to comprehend the human situation is supplanted by the presuppositions of the social engineer, the qualified optimism of the technician supplants the tragic sense of life so close to the heart of the classic drama, and, as Gabriel Marcel has so perceptively stated, the deepest conflicts of the human experience, so long consigned to the domain of literary wonder and religious mystery, have optimistically emerged (if not quite to the liking of us all) into the sunny realm of "solvable problems."

Like Marcel, I could illustrate this shift with many examples, but I shall choose only one as the latest source of my own dismay. In a course in nineteenth century philosophy we study Tolstoy and read his famous novel *Anna Karenina*. One student whom I asked to report on Tolstoy's philosophy as expressed in that book replied confidently that, so far as he could see, whatever philosophy expressed there was irrelevant. The real point, he said, was the antiquated divorce law of Czarist Russia. Had this been reformed, there would have been no need and no occasion for Tolstoy to write the book at all! This is the social engineering mentality at its provoking best, and it indicates what the humanities have to gain from that scientific and technological understanding which would plan for our happiness, correct the world by science, and guide our lives by information.

The aims of education in general, and the aims of education in the humanities in particular, are to be understood in terms of the social context within which they arise, and they gain clarity when the goals of their society are also transparent and understood. But a general fogginess about the latter prevents the clarity of the former, which, as protagonists of the humanities, we should certainly like. Even in the absence of such clear formulation, however, it is possible from the very history of the humanities to discern the role which they have played in previous cultures and the heritage which they have transmitted to the present age with its vastly different sociological conditions and cultural needs. Something of this sense of discrepancy between prior tasks and present expectations has been at the root of all that I have wished to suggest in this lecture about the relationship of humanistic effort to cultural milieu. For if this relationship can be reasonably illuminated, this can also help us to make connections between the current criticism of the humanities and the disillusionment out of which it has so often sprung.

My lecture yesterday began with some of the dilemmas set for us by C. P. Snow in *The Two Cultures and the Scientific Revolution*, and its dramatization of the not always good natured opposition between the humanities and the sciences. Snow, as I intimated, for all that he is a novelist of talent, is, I am afraid, ideologically no friend of the humanities. One possible reason is suggested by what I have said this morning. In the first place, as one who has passed through, and perhaps suffered from, the English system of education, he has probably felt the legacy of Jebb and Jowett—the aristocratic spirit which has so often seemed but the most arrant snobbery to those not immediately born to the Establishment. If this is so, we have a living demonstration of how the seeds of aristocratic self-sufficiency in the nineteenth century British university have weakened the prestige of the humanities today. The arrogance of nineteenth century Oxford means that in our own time the humanities are often at a disadvantage against a scientific education which has none of the class implications of the former.

But democracy, science, and the facts of a late Alexandrian life are not the only considerations which qualify humanistic effectiveness. The humanities are also exposed to cosmopolitan expectations of an immensity which calls into question the whole narrow conception of our previous educational ambitions. Of course the Platonic educational ideal has been of immense service throughout the course of European civilization.

> His type of culture [as Whitehead said] is the peculiar inspiration of the liberal aristocrat, the class from which Europe derives what ordered liberty it now possesses. For centuries, from Pope Nicholas V to the school of the Jesuits, and from the Jesuits to the modern headmasters of English public schools, this educational ideal has had the strenuous support of the clergy. For certain people it is a very good education. It suits their type of mind and the circumstances amid which their life is passed. But more has been claimed for it than this. All education has been judged adequate or defective according to its approximation to this sole type.[32]

And he continues by showing, not unlike Snow himself, how the expression of the human spirit is not confined to literature and how the sciences and the technologies make their own rightful claims.

The age of the gentleman is perhaps gone forever, and the age of the professional has now conclusively taken its place, but the humanities, in adapting to this transformation, need not automatically rush to embrace the questionable blessings of science. There are, I know, those who have welcomed what they call "the knowledge explosion in the humanities," and who have called for a welcoming attitude to the computer, as well as mathematical and statistical theory, as brilliant tools which present-day technology has provided for handling masses of humanistic material.[33] But I doubt that the wisdom and self-understanding for which our modern cultural situation cries out will be the product of their mechanical processing. If it comes, it will come through other and more humane instrumentalities.

In my lecture this morning I have tried to suggest less dogmatically than dialectically some of the threats and dangers, the stresses and strains, with which the humanities are confronted in the modern world. I have spoken of the fragility of our survival, the dangers of looking backward, the aristocratic temptation, the narrow nationalistic possibility. But I have emphasized no less the strain of a new inclusiveness, the dangers of cosmopolitanism, the loss of myth, and the threat of the rationalistic mentality of science. These are threats and dangers which are inherent in our present cultural situation, and they admit of no facile resolution. It has not been my intention to pretend to solve them once and for all, for this, I freely confess, is beyond my modest powers. I have simply tried to insert them once again into that continuing debate which must be a primary concern of all those whose deepest wish it is that we shall share a common humanistic future.

5 ❖ Ultimate Aims

IF, AS I HAVE SUGGESTED IN MY FIRST LECTURE, THE HUMAN-
ITIES BE CONSIDERED IDENTICAL WITH THE LIBERAL ARTS AND
if these latter are, for practical purposes, conceived as the arts of
communication, the arts of continuity, and the arts of criticism,
then the prima facie aim of the humanities is implicit in the
very disciplines they comprise. Language, we have not had to
wait for the instruction of Wittgenstein and his followers to in-
form us, is the matrix of our existence, the foundation of human
sociality, and the elementary condition of our literary expressiveness. But nonetheless Wittgenstein put it well: "Und eine Sprache
vorstellen heisst, sich eine Lebensform vorstellen." (And to imagine a language means to imagine a form of life.)[34]

Many classicists deplore the passing of that time in the history of western culture when the two languages, Greek and Latin,
and their respective literatures, formed the kernel of humanistic
instruction. They were not living languages; to be sure, they were
preeminently "literary." But in the examination of their specimens of consciously literary art, it was hoped that they, through
an initial aesthetic appeal, would humanize and develop those
upon whom their impulse was thrust—educate their taste, form
their character, increase their sensitivity to values, to the Greek
feeling for beauty and the moral virtues of the Romans. These
two languages and the literatures they comprised gave a sense of
manageability to the extant cultural heritage. Their literary, historical, and philosophical masterpieces were limited in number,
and for a long period in western history, the Latin language, at
least, was a token of universality—a shared presupposition for the
discourse of the intellectual leaders of the western world. It is said

that Erasmus, citizen of the world, could converse in no other language, Descartes' chief works had to be translated from the Latin into French, and the universality of the language of scientific thought is indicated by the fact that exactly a hundred years after England's greatest poet Shakespeare was writing his *Hamlet* in English, her greatest scientist Newton was writing his *Principia* in Latin.

From one point of view, therefore, the rise of the vernacular languages and literatures introduced an inevitable provincialism into western civilization. National language as experienced language tends to become personal, to assimilate within its usages all of the affective values of childhood and early youth, and this can serve as a limitation upon the universality of essentially abstract notions. But it can be a virtue too, since it is in this way primarily that, in Wittgenstein's sense, language becomes "a form of life." To restrict discourse to a single language is a severe limitation upon the imagination, and in a world ever growing in its interconnectedness, but at the same time increasingly threatened by the incomprehension between competing and yet coexisting cultures, the classicist prejudice constitutes, as we have seen, a diminution, an impoverishment, and a danger. To imagine and to sympathize with "forms of life" other than our own becomes an obligation and a necessity. In a world expanded to the very limits of cultural divergence and ideological antagonism, the arts of communication need no extrinsic justification of their utility.

In the same way the arts of continuity need little in the way of justification. Since the days when Herodotus recorded the great Persian war of invasion, but did so in a fashion as to equally acquaint the Greeks with their own earlier history and with a knowledge of the kind of people in their surrounding world with which they had to deal, since the days when Thucydides wrote the history of the Peloponnesian war (as he hoped) in a fashion which should be equally acceptable to both the victor and the defeated and, thus, by a crystallization of experience, to heal the wounds of memory, the social function of historiography has been an accepted principle. Obscured as it may have been by the purely intellectual impulse and by the obsessive urge to turn the humanities into social sciences, so characteristic alike of eighteenth century British common sense and nineteenth century Prussian exactitude, it has never been completely lost from view. For it has always been unconsciously understood that the basic problem of any society is to consolidate its members into one communal fellowship. On an elementary level this implies a common set of cultural habits and social responses, but on a deeper and more significant level it implies a common emotional and intellectual development, and, above all, a common matrix of values. But the first requirement for a common emotional and intellectual development among men, as well as the first requirement in order that they may have a common matrix of values, is that *they must enjoy a common past*. To provide this common past is the first phase of the unique social function of the humanities understood as the arts of continuity.[35] And here it is a matter not only of history proper but also of the classics of literature, philosophy, and history taken as a repository of historical values and the witnesses of cultural continuity. By conserving and continually re-presenting the intellectual and cultural heritage of human civilization, the humanities serve to initiate youth into a society which is broader than the factory and the legislature, the computer center and the commission of administrative experts, and to make them members of a truly common universe of discourse. In this respect the arts of communication and continuity can have no choice but to take the classics as their subject matter. To relive the tradition from the Bhagavad-Gita to Proust, from Confucius to Whitehead, and from the Chou bronzes to the Bauhaus is their inescapable obligation.

It should be noted that I have spoken of the cultural heritage of *human* civilization and not simply that of western culture. For, as I pointed out yesterday, the effective range of humanistic concern has outrun the European heartland to encompass the world. This has had its effect upon the newer conception of the required range of history in the West. The cosmopolitan efforts of Spengler and Toynbee to overcome the Ptolemaic blindness of a Europe-centered historiography have born fruits, and if the efforts of the former to construct a morphology of world history are now seen as a merely quaint prescientific effort and if the attempt of the latter to predict a new syncretic religion (in which the insights of

Christianity, Mahayana Buddhism, Hinduism, and Mohamme-
danism coalesce) seems only bizarre, yet it is no longer possible
to return to the ideals of historiography in the nineteenth century
tradition. Ranke's bland assumption that *history* means the history of the great European powers and Treitschke's even more
fanatical attempt to write history "exclusively for Germans," as
he said, and in the service of the Prussian State, belong to a
bygone age.

The sense of the historical horizon has immeasurably broad-
ened, and its consequences are to be seen even in the prosaic field
of the elementary texts. I have before me as I write two examples:
one by Professor L. S. Stavrianos of Northwestern entitled *The
World Since 1500: A Global History* published by Prentice-Hall
in 1966; the other by Professor William H. McNeill of the University of Chicago entitled *A World History* published by Oxford
University Press in 1967. Both works were subsidized by the
Carnegie Corporation. Both works witness the impact of Spengler
and Toynbee. Both works are a return to the ideals of the Enlightenment, when for a brief moment the ideas of "humanity"
and "mankind" lighted up the dark obsessive nationalism of an
emerging Europe. Both are addressed to the newer historical tasks
of a cosmopolitan age.

Reference to the Enlightenment reminds me that a perfect
rationale for the values which lie at the foundation of the arts of
continuity and communication is to be found in the philosopher
who most quintessentially expressed its dominant attitudes, Immanuel Kant. It is in a little-remarked passage from his *Critique
of Judgment*.

> The propaedeutic to all beautiful art, regarded in the highest
> degree of its perfection, seems to lie not in precepts, but in the
> culture of the mental powers by means of those elements of
> knowledge called *humaniora*, probably because *humanity* on the
> one side indicates the universal *feeling of sympathy*, and on the
> other the faculty of being able to *communicate* universally our
> inmost feelings. For these properties taken together constitute the
> characteristic social spirit of humanity by which it is distinguished
> from the limitations of animal life.[36]

Here is distinct recognition that the humanities, especially as
embodied in the masterworks of literature, philosophy, and his-

tory, rest upon the feeling of sympathy and the ability to communicate this feeling universally. It is the universality of the great books which certifies to their indispensibility in the consolidation of a cosmopolitan tradition.

The above passage from Kant is immediately followed by one even more advanced for its time. Kant has been speaking of an historical age which faces the difficult problem of uniting freedom and equality with respect and the sense of duty, and he continues:

> Such an age and such a people naturally first found out the art of reciprocal communication of ideas between the cultivated and uncultivated classes and thus discovered how to harmonize the large-mindedness and refinement of the former with the natural simplicity and originality of the latter. In this way they first found that mean between the higher culture and simple nature which furnishes that true standard for taste as a sense common to all men which no universal rules can supply.[37]

It is a passage which admits the class division within society but reluctantly, and looks forward to the moment when large-mindedness and refinement can be joined to simplicity and originality in that harmony which only a democratic synthesis can provide. In these passages from Kant we find support for the humanities in one of their ultimate aims.

The social function of the humanities is to unify society through the development of a common emotional and intellectual framework within its individual members. But in order that this unification should itself be legitimate, two preconditions are necessary. The first is that the society in question be transregional and transnational in scope. The second is that such acculturation as the humanities provide be available for all without economic or social class restrictions. Only in their denial of the nationalistic and the aristocratic, only in their affirmation of the democratic and universal values, are the humanities deserving of that future which their present crisis leaves open to doubt.

The third of the liberal arts, the art of criticism, or philosophy, also carries its legitimation in its own nature. But I should want to make clear that in speaking of philosophy in this fashion, I am not identifying it with the more analytical type of philosophizing which is so popular today and which has the deepest mistrust for speculation and the great metaphysical systems. My meaning does not stem from C. D. Broad's distinction between critical and speculative philosophy (with an obvious preference for the former), but rather from the last chapter of Dewey's *Experience and Nature*, which is entitled "Existence, Value and Criticism."[38] For the crux of Dewey's argument here is the very simple one that criticism is the instrument for the discernment of value.

Deploring the frequently sharp separation between a "realm of values" and the "sphere of ordinary existence," Dewey emphasizes the uses of criticism in finding the former in the latter, that is to say, in refusing to accept the Platonic strategy of separation, but instead, of so discriminating among "goods" on the basis of their appearances and their consequences that they may be maximized. In recognizing, with Dewey, that philosophy is inherently criticism and meaning by *criticism* discriminating judgment, careful appraisal, or rational evaluation as the intelligent inquiry into the conditions and consequences of value objects, we shift the value preoccupation of the humanities from the substantive to the procedural. "Teaching values" thus means less either a dogmatic assertion or a repetitive fixation of affective-volitional meanings (which with the best will in the world might be called propaganda rather than education) than *practice in the art of discrimination*, and this shift has the virtue that it makes no absolutely sharp separation of the acts of analysis, appreciation, and criticism from one another, but finds them, all three, continuous moments of a valuational (and evaluational) activity at the very heart of humanistic concern. Cultivated taste—surely one of the ultimate aims of the humanities in their aesthetic dimension—is capable of the sustained appreciation of masterpieces of literature and works of art precisely because it is the consequence of long training in the uncovering of affective meanings in aesthetic objects where appreciation and criticism are both part of a single rhythmic cycle, and it is probable that conscience in moral behavior is developed in the course of an analogous critical consideration of alternatives in an ongoing process in which the performance of acts alternates with episodes of moral deliberation.

Philosophic discourse functions for Dewey much as literary discourse functions for Matthew Arnold—it is a "criticism of life" —a comment upon experience in the interest of a more intense and valid appreciation of the affective-volitional meanings which it contains. Its ultimate aim is to clarify, make available, and extend these meanings or values in the service of a richer and more productive life. It is in this way that the arts of criticism also have direct relevance to the problems of man in society, for it is their role to criticize accepted beliefs, cherished customs and institutions, and to propose policies, conventional or utopian, as they bear upon the achievement of future good. "Social reform," says Dewey, "is conceived in a Philistine spirit, if it is taken to mean anything less than precisely the liberation and expansion of the meanings of which experience is capable."[39]

This means that the arts of criticism are never separable from the social context in which they originate nor from the antecedently given problems to which they address themselves. The arts precede aesthetic judgment, and habitual social behavior precedes ethical theory. For the purpose of criticism, whether aesthetically or morally oriented, is to make aesthetic judgments and moral choices reflectively and under the guidance of rational criteria, rather than blindly under the influence of impulse or whim. Philosophy, as I have defined it elsewhere, is thus nothing but *a reflection upon the varieties of experience.*[40]

So far, I have examined the ultimate aims of the humanities as the ultimate aims intrinsic to the liberal arts with which I have identified them—the arts of communication, the arts of continuity, and the arts of criticism. In the case of the arts of communication this has meant the presentation of languages as forms of life enlarging a limited imagination and producing that mutual sympathy which Kant took to be the defining property of social man. In the case of the arts of continuity, comprehending both history proper and the use of the classics of literature and philosophy, presented as elements in a continuous human tradition, this has meant the presentation of a common past in the service of social cohesiveness and enlarged social sensitivity. And finally, in the case of the arts of criticism, this has meant the enlargement of the faculty of criticism, philosophically conceived as intelligent inquiry into the nature and maximization of values. A humane imagination, the forging of a universal social bond based upon sympathy, and the inculcation of a technique for the realization of values then become the ultimate goals of the liberal arts. This seems simple enough, but the history of the humanities has not always seen it this way.

For example, the conception of the arts of criticism presented above visualizes them as analytic—even "factual"—rather than frankly dogmatic, hortatory, or prescriptive. And this seems to run counter to a long and established tradition which finds the humanistic classics directly educational in a prescriptive sense, exemplary, that is, of values which, once open to inspection, make an immediate, almost intuitive claim to acceptance. This tradition, too, probably originates in the strong moralistic bias of Roman rhetorical concerns, but its most notable examples in our history come in the Renaissance with its revival of the Roman cultural claims.

Typical is the case of Erasmus and his *Institio principis Christiani* (Education for a Christian Prince) of 1516.[41] Written when he enjoyed the honorary position of councillor to the youthful Charles V, it was another of those Renaissance treatises on royal education elicited by the conviction that political improvement in the state was a function of the moral transformation of the prince and based upon a firm faith in the power of the classics to mold character and direct practice. In this faith Erasmus is the child of his time and the very epitome of Renaissance humanism. In a similar fashion, for Machiavelli, too, Livy was a crucial source of political wisdom, and Montaigne, speaking of the work of Tacitus, could say, "It is a nursery of ethical and political reflections for the provision and adornment of those who hold a place in the management of the world."[42] But Erasmus differed from both Machiavelli and Montaigne in two important respects. His emphasis is ethical and religious rather than pragmatic and worldly, and he therefore favors the Christian and the Greek sources over the Roman, the moral philosophers over the historians. For those who believe that the humanities are a direct source for the inculcation of moral values, Erasmus' *Education of a Christian Prince* is worthy of sustained attention. He would have his Prince read *Proverbs* and *Ecclesiastes*, the *Lives* and *Moralia* of Plutarch, Aristotle's *Politics* and Cicero's *Offices*, but above all the works of Plato. Against the Greek historians (Herodotus and Xenophon) one must be on guard—they are pagans and often set forth the worst type of prince—and the Romans (Sallust and Livy) are hardly any better. Although for humanism the ability of classical literature to serve for moral and political education was, as I have said, an article of faith, already there is no easy agreement as to what the precise content of that education should be, and Machiavelli's favor for Livy, Montaigne's for Tacitus and Plutarch, and Erasmus' for the Old Testament and Plato, already indicates a battleground for the competing claims of alternative moral values. But that such moral values exist, and that their direct inculcation is possible through the humanities, was never in doubt.

This tradition has a long history from Erasmus to our own day. That imaginative literature, philosophy, and the arts and history of the classical world can somehow serve to train the value-consciousness has been a constant claim, and it recurs in some of the most unexpected places. It is in Schiller's belief in the theater as a moral institution, in the possibility of "the aesthetic education of man" (which in his hands is so largely moral) and in the combination of the two in his belief that the political drama can be used as a tool of "the political and educating artist" (*der pädagogischen und politischen Künstler*).[43] It is in Jacob Burckhardt's passionate conviction that education in the classical heritage of the Graeco-Roman and the Renaissance past would somehow provide authentic values to compensate for the failures of bourgeois commercialism and materialism. And it is, strangely enough, also in the belief of the great Marxist literary critic Georg Lukacs, whose whole later life has been one passionate attempt to substitute the influence of the great "realists" like Shakespeare, Molière, Balzac, and Tolstoy for that of their "decadent" adversaries Flaubert, Rilke, Kafka, and Proust.[44] Throughout this tradition also the function of the humanities to directly inculcate values has been an enduring presupposition.

In speaking of the tradition which believes that the humanities serve to directly inculcate substantive values, I find that I have constantly used the terms *conviction*, *faith*, and *presupposi-*

tion. Surely this is not enough. Conviction must be justified. Faith must be securely based. Presuppositions, when challenged, must legitimize their claim. There is considerable disillusionment with the humanities today, and it in no small part springs from the uneasiness of those who feel that they (the humanities) have not justified this conviction, firmly based this faith, or legitimized this claim. C. P. Snow's charge that humanists are hopelessly conservative, insensitive to contemporary values, absolutely unmoved by their current social responsibilities, and that by contrast, it is the scientists who "are by and large the soundest group of intellectuals we have" is one instance of this disillusionment. William Arrowsmith's tendentious claim that the current humanities are "in sorry shape" because of a "professionalism" which neglects values for the cult of objectivity and the emulation of scientific exactitude is another. And, at the risk of indiscretion, I myself must say that when I read the lurid claims made for the humanities both in the *Report of the Commission on the Humanities* and on the floor of Congress and contrast them with much of present example and practice of scholarship and teaching in the humanities, I sometimes feel apprehension lest our claims be investigated by some cosmic Better Business Bureau.

> All men [asserts the *Report*] require that a vision be held before them, an ideal toward which they may strive. Americans need such a vision today as never before in their history. It is both the dignity and the duty of humanists to offer their fellow-countrymen whatever understanding can be attained by fallible humanity of such enduring values as justice, freedom, virtue, beauty, and truth. Only thus do we join ourselves to the heritage of our nation and our human kind.
>
> Democracy demands wisdom of the average man. Without the exercise of wisdom free institutions and personal liberty are inevitably imperiled. To know the best that has been thought and said in former times can make us wiser than we otherwise might be, and in this respect the humanities are not merely our, but the world's best hope.[45]

Can make us wiser than we otherwise might be—aye, there's the rub—*can* make us wiser, but not necessarily *does* make us wiser, and when one compares the "duty of humanists to offer their fellow-men understanding of such values as justice, freedom, virtue, beauty, and truth" with some of the projects submitted to the National Council of the Humanities for support, such as "An index to the Maggs Brothers catalogues" or "The British elocutionary movement and its influence upon American philology" or "A cost analysis of the building of the Strozzi palace" or "The substitute aria in Italian Opera Seria between 1700-1740" or "The locating of ancient Hebrew documents in secreted Spanish vaults" or "The interaction of the employees who operated trains on American railroads with their society, 1865-1900" or "The relationship between verbal types and choice of objective pronoun forms in contemporary Spanish" or "An ethnic research survey of Northwest Indiana" or "An investigation of certain locutions of visual perception tangential to the 'seeing as' locution" or "A study of the financial account books of Charles Dickens' publishers," then one shares some of C. P. Snow's disillusionment and William Arrowsmith's aggressive despair.

The point here is partly the matter of questionable humanistic relevance, but it is also the divorce between the "meaning" and the adjectives "affective-volitional" in my characterization of values as *affective-volitional meanings* in my second lecture. And we return to the problem that was suggested there. To make one acquainted with values as meanings is an intellectual enterprise alone, but to "teach values" in the effective sense would mean to transmit an emotional dynamic through contagion—something like Arrowsmith's "personal influence and personal example" —and to instill a sense of obligation toward the maximization of values themselves. Are the humanities capable of undertaking this responsibility with success?

The problem can be put in a simpler way. If there has been considerable confusion about the value competence of the humanities, it is because there has not always been sufficient clarity in distinguishing three things: (1) the humanities, (2) humanitarian values, and (3) the humanistic attitude. For what is often passed over with obstinacy, if not with arrogance, is the fact that *there is no automatic relationship between the first and the second two.* The studies which I have spoken of as the liberal arts— the arts of communication, continuity, and criticism, the languages and literatures, history, and philosophy—have not always been taught, and in some instances *are not now being taught* in such a way as either to further the values of justice and compassion or to stress the organic, the qualitative, and the human as against the factual, the quantitative, and the mechanical.

This is a serious matter both theoretically and practically. For there is a standing complaint among teachers and researchers in the humanities that they are the stepchildren of modern education. There seems unquestionably to be a greater relative growth in other areas of learning—the natural and the social sciences particularly—and in a society obsessed with the concept of "growth rate," this can be a matter for grave concern. The relative decline in humanistic progress is felt in three areas: in the number of students enrolled in the humanities, in their quality, and in the financial support available for humanistic research. As the *Report* of 1964 announced with some shrillness: "We must unquestionably increase the prestige of the humanities and the flow of funds to them." For the basic explanation put forward by the humanities themselves for their decline is the unwarranted relative prestige of the sciences and the relatively unmerited increase in financial support which they enjoy. This explanation has been disputed with disturbing logic in a recent article by W. David Maxwell, Professor of Business Economics at Indiana University, entitled "A Methodological Hypothesis for the Plight of the Humanities,"[46] and I should like to turn for a moment to its argument.

It is simple. The goals of the humanities are high, but we have no evidence that they are furthered by the study of the humanities. What is the nature of the link between the subject matter of the humanities and the aims they profess? We do not really know, and from our ignorance stems the "plight" of the humanities!

> There is thus [says Maxwell] a methodological hiatus between the humanities and the goals of the humanities. We cannot objectively specify the subject-matter which will further these goals because we cannot specify *how* it does so. We can only assert *that* it does. Because of this methodological gap, research in the humanities often lacks purpose and direction. Since we do not

know the process by which the goals of the humanities are furthered, we often cannot screen out those research efforts which make little or no contribution to this end from those that contribute significantly. For this same reason, there are often no set criteria with which to judge the method used in research or its results.[47]

This may seem to be a simple case of a social scientist missing the point—of his attempt to apply quantitative criteria in an area where such application is intrinsically inappropriate. What is moral sensitivity? What is aesthetic taste? What exactly is wisdom? These questions elude quantitative determination, although we can identify them in those instances when we ourselves are morally sensitive, aesthetically competent, and wise. But I think Maxwell means more than this. Unconsciously, he too, I think, is disturbed by the problematic relationship between the humanities as subjects and the humanitarian values and the humanistic attitude which it should be their business to foster and promote. And this becomes evident in his final point.

> Thus there is a possibility that the crisis in the humanities is not that society has failed to increase *pari passu* the resources devoted to them but that they have incorrectly defined the soul of our culture so that they now have relatively less to tell us about the total cultural setting in which man finds himself. That the goals of the humanities encompass some which are perhaps more vital to our survival than any of those of the natural sciences may only mean that the humanities' relatively decreased ability to further their goal is the greatest tragedy of all.[48]

What is at stake here is a sense of the irrelevance of humanistic knowledge, a suggestion that the centers of power have shifted because the promise once so glowingly held out by humanists has not been fulfilled and that the new promise is in the hands of an applied social science. Ithiel de Sola Pool has already intimated as much: that just as the humanists were once expected to train the prince, now they have been supplanted by the social scientists for the training of the mandarins; that in an age when the role of the intellectual was to uphold the *status quo*, it was permissible, even strategic, to look back to Livy and to Tacitus, the Old Testament and Plato, but that now when his role is to "unmask ideology" and to "criticize society," the conventional wisdom will no longer do, and a radical knowledge of manipulation and control—the stock in trade of the behavioral sciences—must take the center of the educational stage.

Although I am deeply concerned that the humanities be held accountable for furthering the humanitarian values and fostering the humanistic attitude and that they fulfill their social function, I simply do not believe that they have become irrelevant, without contemporary meaning, forced to yield present place to the applied social sciences. I do not deny the utility of the latter, but in the modern world it is precisely words like "manipulation" and "control" which are frightening, and it is just the humanistic emphasis upon "freedom" and "reflection" and "personal responsibility" which is perhaps the only antidote to their poison. It may be true, as I did indeed suggest in my third lecture, that the aristocratic temptation is one to which the humanities once succumbed and which they must now vigorously resist; but that they have been eternally ideological rather than utopian in Mannheim's sense —backward-looking and acceptant of society as it was, rather than dangerously forward-looking and idealistic—is a charge which cannot be substantiated. Not that I believe this to be the crucial issue with respect to the humanities, but simply taken on its own terms, it is necessary to point out that Euripides, Dante, Occam, Thomas More, Bacon, Galileo, Descartes, Rousseau, Hume, Buechner, Baudelaire, Thoreau, and Marx were radical for their time, and in some instances and respects remain so for ours.

What I do think is valuable about current attacks upon the humanities is that they will prevent us from simply taking our work for granted. The "conviction," the "faith," the "presupposition" that the humanities teach values is not enough. They must be taught with this constant aim in mind and with an experimental willingness at every point to explore the actual relationships between the content of the liberal arts and the humanitarian values and the humanistic attitude which are their reasons for existence, their card of accreditation in the spectrum of teaching and research.

That we must be more concerned and responsible is true. But talk about the humanities being outmoded among the newer tasks of the natural and the social sciences makes no sense either. It is but a part of the stylistic faddishness which strikes the learned world from time to time, taking its clue from the new and dramatic prominence of some aspect of society—generally technological—like the monstrous growth of the mass media or the appearance of nuclear fission, and finding its mouthpieces in genuinely concerned, but often woefully mistaken, culture heroes like Marshall McLuhan and C. P. Snow.

The humanities cannot be dismissed. Far from being outmoded, they are eternally relevant precisely because they are the arts of communication, the arts of continuity, and the arts of criticism. Language remains the indispensible medium within which we move and breathe. History provides that group memory which makes the communal bond possible. Philosophic criticism is the only activity through which man's self-reflection modifies the conditions of his existence. The cup of the humanities, therefore, must be the vessel from which we drink our life.

NOTES

1. Perhaps the best brief account of the development of the liberal arts is still Paul Abelson, *The Seven Liberal Arts* (New York: Teachers College, Columbia University, 1906).

2. See, for example, the rather elaborate treatment of W. T. Jones in *The Sciences and the Humanities* (Berkeley: University of California Press, 1965).

3. Alfred North Whitehead, "Harvard: The Future," *Atlantic Monthly*, September, 1936, and Robert M. Hutchins, "A Reply to Professor Whitehead," *Atlantic Monthly*, November, 1936. My own attempt to evaluate what precisely was at stake appeared a year later: Albert William Levi, "The Problem of Higher Education: Whitehead and Hutchins," *The Harvard Educational Review*, October, 1937.

4. Characteristic is the British collection: *Crisis in the Humanities*, edited by J. H. Plumb (Penguin Books, 1964).

5. Albert William Levi, *Literature, Philosophy and the Imagination* (Bloomington: Indiana University Press, 1962).

6. L. J. Paetow, *The Arts Course at Mediaeval Universities* (Champaign, Illinois, 1910).

7. Edward Kennard Rand, *Founders of the Middle Ages* (Cambridge: Harvard University Press, 1929).

8. J. Bronowski, *Science and Human Values* (New York: Harper Torchbooks, 1959), pp. 14, 65, 90.

9. Rand, pp. 147, 148.

10. Ludwig Wittgenstein, *Philosophical Investigations* (New York: Macmillan, 1953), Sec. 65–67.

11. Northrup Frye, *Anatomy of Criticism* (New York: Atheneum, 1967), p. 12.

12. George Santayana, *Scepticism and Animal Faith* (New York: Scribner's, 1924), p. ix.

13. Immanuel Kant, *Kritik der Reinen Vernunft* (Hamburg: Felix Meiner, 1952), pp. 753–54.

14. *Transport to Summer* (New York: Knopf, 1947), p. 87.

15. *The Cantos of Ezra Pound* (New Directions, 1948), pp. 63–64.

16. *Congressional Record*: House Proceedings, February 27, 1968.

17. "The Shame of the Graduate Schools," *Harpers,* March, 1966.

18. *Report of the Commission on the Humanities* (The American Council of Learned Societies, 1964), p. 1.

19. Michael Polanyi, *Personal Knowledge* (New York: Harper Torchbooks, 1964).

20. Arrowsmith.

21. C. P. Snow, *The Two Cultures and the Scientific Revolution* (New York: Cambridge University Press, 1962).

22. Bronowski.

23. Albert William Levi, *Philosophy and the Modern World* (Bloomington: Indiana University Press, 1959), Chaps. VIII, XII.

24. George Santayana, *Interpretations of Poetry and Religion* (New York: Harper Torchbooks, 1957), pp. 2–3.

25. *The Necessary Angel* (New York: Knopf, 1951), p. 36.

26. *Bacon's Advancement of Learning* (Oxford World Classics, 1929), p. 90.

27. Gilbert Ryle, *Dilemmas* (Cambridge University Press, 1954), p. 1.

28. George Santayana, *Dialogues In Limbo* (New York: Scribner's, 1925), p. 75.

29. *History and Politics* (New York: Pantheon Books, 1962), p. 23.

30. Friedrich Nietzsche, *Die Geburt der Tragödie* (Leipzig: C. G. Naumann, 1894), p. 130.

31. Ibid., pp. 160–61.

32. Alfred North Whitehead, *The Aims of Education and Other Essays* (New York: The Free Press, 1967), p. 46.

33. For example, Walter J. Ong, "The Expanding Humanities and the Individual Scholar," *P.M.L.A.*, September, 1967.

34. Sec. 19.

35. The ideas here were first put forward in Albert William Levi, "The Social Function of the Humanities," *The Educational Forum*, May, 1942. This essay was written under the goad of totalitarianism and the Second World War, but I find it still valid, and much of it is incorporated into this lecture.

36. *Kritik der Urteilskraft* (Hamburg: Felix Meiner, 1959), p. 216.

37. Ibid.

38. John Dewey, *Experience and Nature* (New York: Norton, 1929).

39. Ibid., p. 411.

40. Albert William Levi, *Varieties of Experience* (New York: Ronald Press, 1957), Chap. I.

41. Desiderius Erasmus, *The Education of a Christian Prince* (New York: Columbia University Press, 1936).

42. *Essais* (Paris: Editions Garnier, 1962), II, 378.

43. *Schillers Werke* in zwei Bänden (Munich: Knaur), II, 570.

44. See Georg Lukacs, *Studies In European Realism* (New York: The Universal Library, 1964), Preface.

45. *Report of the Commission on the Humanities*, p. 4.

46. *Bulletin of the American Association of University Professors*, March, 1968.

47. Ibid., p. 82.

48. Ibid., p. 84.